COME, DRINK "DEEP" OF
LIVING WATERS

Come, Drink "Deep" of Living Waters

Faith Seeking Understanding in the Twenty-First Century

BARBARA FIAND

A Crossroad Book
The Crossroad Publishing Company

The Crossroad Publishing Company
www.CrossroadPublishing.com
© 2016 by Barbara Fiand

Book design by The HK Scriptorium

Library of Congress Cataloging-in-Publication Data
available from the Library of Congress.

ISBN 978-0-8245-2196-7

Books published by The Crossroad Publishing Company may be pur-chased at special quantity discount rates for classes and institutional use. For information, please e-mail sales@CrossroadPublishing.com

In appreciation for
The Leadership Conference of Women Religious,
their model of leadership, dedication, and passion,
their search for justice and for truth

Contents

1

On Living in a Time
of Bridging

We are planetary people. Our security is the sun around which we travel—always passing again where we already were. Yet, even though it would appear that circular travel is like an eternal return and gets us nowhere, in an omnicentric universe that is at every moment expanding from every point, we are also always moving beyond ourselves and our presumed securities into the yet unknown. The reality of our planetary existence, of its illusory stability in a universe that actually is in perpetual transformation, seems to me a powerful symbol for the growth and profound conversion all of us are called to at this time in human history

We live in a "time of bridging" that invites us to learn, and then to accept with utmost respect, that what has provided us with a certain wisdom and security for several thousand years of movement around our star is today ebbing away and has, in fact, done so for at least a century or more. A "time of bridging" involves allowing for this realization and, with serenity, courage, and trust, seeking the footprints revealing who has walked among us unobserved all this time. Today this realization is lighting up with ever greater brilliance and being recognized and acknowledged with ever more urgency due to our scientific discoveries and spiritual insights. Its irresistible lure is challenging us to surrender both to the pathos as well as to the excitement that can no longer be ignored or even repressed by anyone who has the courage to see.

It seems to me that as spiritual beings, we are today, perhaps more so than at any other time in history, becoming aware of the fact that in our very essence *we are a pilgrim people*, and that *our ecstasy is in the journey.* A strange paradox reveals itself with this insight, for even as we yearn for stability and home, we find ourselves stretched beyond ourselves to a destiny yet unknown. It would seem that this destiny and our arrival can only be attained in the serenity that allows what *is,* to *be*; that surrenders to the Ultimate in its *unfolding.* We are homecoming-on-the-way. Many years ago, in my very first book, *Releasement: Spirituality for Ministry,* I suggested that "We are pilgrims," and that "Our home is the heart of God." Today, over thirty years later, I am ever more aware that the infinite expanse of divinity makes pilgrimage an eternal reality. Is not this the ecstasy, the allure?

The Need for Bridging

In the light of these thoughts, the challenges facing a faith seeking understanding in the twenty-first century are not only overwhelming but, indeed, most urgent. We live in a time of extraordinary discoveries in both outer space and quantum "space-less-ness," a time of depth explorations into human consciousness, as well as into the broader reality of cosmic consciousness. Today, influences on human behavior from the farthest as well as the most intimate sources imaginable are recognized, taken seriously, and explored by the scientific and scholarly community worldwide. At the same time, however, we belong to a church whose governmental structure and creeds belong, at best, to the third, fourth, or fifth century with some minor changes and even greater strictures along the way—always careful not to disturb the "deposit of faith" handed down in an ancient language and codified in a context that, for the most part, has totally lost its meaning in our day.

I am aware of a deep ache inside me as I am writing this. Most Catholics, and perhaps members of some other Christian denominations as well, were reared in a religious culture that blindly embraced this structure and the context in which it was created hundreds or even thousands of years ago. For Catholics, doubting what was taught in religion classes was considered a serious sin. It was expected that we memorize the creed, and questioning what it declared was unheard of. I was brought up with this conviction, and so, during my years of growing up, I simply "swallowed hard" and refused to think about the factual nature of faith proclamations; about the reality of its metaphors, myths, or parables presented as history. Like many Catholics of my time, I love my church and have loved the stories of my faith. In the beginning, I tried hard to bracket the ancient interpretations connected to them and to shield myself from the pain of critique and reinterpretation. As the years went by, however, I found that, much as I may have wanted to, I could no longer do that without contextualizing and "demythologizing" what I read, nor could I simply accept the dogmatic certitudes formulated in response to scripture stories. I began to realize, much to my sorrow, that Catholicism's resistance to and fear of, as well as past persecutions, of science in general were rooted in the challenges its discoveries posed to these ancient certitudes. Even today's seeming alarm about and objection to the theory of "conscious evolution" on the part of the Congregation for the Doctrine of the Faith (CDF) seem to be caught in this dilemma.

Authentic maturation for individuals, cultures, as well as religions, inevitably makes demands on all of us. The "living waters" of faith cannot be static forever without growing stale. "Drinking" into their depths demands a constant transformation of our understanding. This can happen only when we allow for the flow of fresh insights that offer themselves to us at every new moment of history. Holding back my fascination with the beauty and excitement of these became, therefore, ever more difficult for me as I matured, especially when I started graduate and post-graduate studies in philosophy and theology. My struggle was exacerbated further when I learned about, and became involved with, the discoveries in science and started to reflect on them in the light of the demands, as well as the prohibitions, of my religion.

Today, research in virtually every discipline is expanding at a pace unheard of in the past. Our assumptions of "facts," therefore, are challenged beyond much of what we simply took for granted even as late as the beginning of the twentieth century and beyond. Would it not make sense then that our earlier attempts at self-knowledge, let alone our thoughts about the universe together with our religious response, should open up to what is being discovered and is revealing itself today? It seems to me that adult faith truly seeking understanding cannot rest but must be ready for ever deeper insights as human questing continues. Saint Paul, in his First Letter to the Corinthians, says it well: "When I was a child, I spoke like a child, I thought like a child, I reasoned like a child; when I became an adult, I put an end to childish ways" (13:11). Our earthly journey into the Mystery is, of course, endless, and Paul readily acknowledges this when he points out that "for now we see through a mirror dimly" (13:12). Seeing only dimly is not an excuse, however, for discouragement, nor for repressing the grace of restlessness given to us from our beginning. It does not absolve us from continuing our "God quest."

What Then Is Truth?

In the light of what we are experiencing today then, it would seem that final certitudes and declarations of *absolute* truths should in all humility be avoided. I believe that this has been difficult to accept, especially for Catholics, ever since Christianity became involved with, and was ultimately "encased," in

Greek metaphysics. The much later theories of the Enlightenment that demanded a factual understanding of the nature of "truth" further exacerbated our obsession with certitude and finality. Today, the humbler view that sees truth more realistically as an evolving relationship between the knower and what *reveals itself* to her or him seems to me much more appropriate. Humans can grasp their reality only according to their intellectual and cultural capacity at any time of their development. A child's truth will change as she or he matures. As we learn from the wisdoms that went before us, and the discoveries that emerge with further research, our understanding expands and our truth evolves. Perhaps more so than ever before, searching today continues on all fronts of human knowing, and faith, finding itself in the midst of this endeavor, needs to respond to the reality of the new and the possibilities of the yet unknown or become obsolete. To paraphrase Wordsworth, "The child is mother of the woman and father of the man." I believe that the woman or man *in* each of us urges and ultimately demands of *our* childhood faith and its longing for truth that it continue to *seek understanding.* Personally, I owe a depth of gratitude for this conviction to those scholars who went, and continue to go, through this process of "seeking understanding" via their various disciplines. They continue to help me along the way to embrace my questing with equanimity and perseverance.

Reflection

As I am reflecting on the struggle that a mature embracing of one's faith entails, I am mindful of the Catholic bishops gathered in Rome for the first session of a synod dealing with the pressing concerns of family life. I am grateful to Pope Francis for calling the leaders of the church to address these issues. Equally well intentioned, surely, was the survey sent from Rome to diocesan bishops throughout the world asking that it be distributed to Catholics in their dioceses for their input prior to the synod. Sadly, however, many of those who answered the survey, especially in the English-speaking world, never received the courtesy of being apprised of its results. It would appear, therefore, that a group of *celibate,* largely ageing men with a disproportionately small group of nonvoting lay persons (a few married couples among them) are gathered in Rome to discuss issues of *married* life. Somehow there is a serious "disconnect" for me in this arrangement, the consequence of which (judging from the German survey results) will very likely be a continued disregard for whatever decisions will be made.

We are told that the discussions in Rome were frank and honest and that some of the ancient prohibitions that hindered free speech in the past were done away with. I am grateful for this. Nevertheless, how is it that those living today's *reality* of family life—of begetting and rearing children, of the economic and (for women) physical hardship in bearing and raising a large number of children—should be expected to accept decisions about *their* life made by men who themselves have absolutely no experience in this regard? How is it, furthermore, that these men can make statements about the perpetuity of marriage mandated by Jesus without seemingly considering the context of the time and the historical circumstances in which this mandate was made? How is it that they can deny table fellowship to those not living up to *their* judgments in this regard? Where in scripture did Jesus ever deny bread to the hungry, table fellowship to sinners? What is *sacred* about regulating who may or may not receive the eucharist? Does it make sense that church law obliges Catholics to attend the eucharistic meal but bars some from partaking of it?

I realize that these are disturbing questions but know that I am certainly not the first contemporary Catholic to raise them. Is not our Catholic governmental structure and its decision-making procedure very similar to those of the last surviving absolute monarchies in the world—just with more "sacred" pageantry? Functioning monarchies in our day and age are generally viewed as oppressive and tyrannical—not terribly different, if at all, from dictatorships. I surmise that they are generally tolerated only where citizens feel powerless to change their country's governing structure. Even the "pomp and circumstance" in public celebrations with monarchical pageantry can wear thin after a while as their out-of-context display evidences their lack of substance.

Catholicism certainly has its "pomp and circumstance" and displays them every time there is a gathering in Rome where decisions will be made for the many by the few. But where is Jesus in all of this, and what is holy about it? The humble carpenter from Palestine must wonder what happened to the movement of transformation he died for. Jesus (who was, and remained, a Jew all his life) spoke of and modeled social and religious transformation. How his teachings have come to be accepted as supporting the structure we have become accustomed to as our church; how we have come to claim it as dating back to him, is a long, arduous, and often cruel story with a variety of interpretations, none of which will be addressed in this book. That it is time, however, for some major change and adaptation is evident. Today, there is no place any longer for triumphalism, for dictates handed down by virtue of appointed office with no need for clarification or rationale except perhaps that "it has always been done that way." As a consequence, *dicta* coming from on high are listened to and followed by an ever-decreasing number of educated Catholics. They have learned to think and to question. They see it as their right to be co-responsible for the church they belong to, the church *they are*. It seems that, in the words of Miriam Therese Winter and her co-authors, Christians (Catholics among them) are "defecting in place." They do not leave the church they love, but they choose to "claim responsibility for their own spiritual lives."[1]

Hope and Gratitude

The purpose of the reflections that follow is to probe some of the major stories of our faith, to reflect on the doctrines attached to them and on some of the rules and ecclesial regulations claiming them as their source. I hope to move deeply and respectfully into contemporary thought and research that might help to contextualize them, and to open up an understanding of them for today. My intention is to do so by primarily giving the end results of present-day research when needed, rather than excessively engaging the reader in the sometimes complex and arduous road scholars need to travel. To do this without dealing with important issues superficially may not always be easy. This book, however, is intended for the general Catholic and Christian reading public who, I believe, is hungry for explanations that, without compromising depth, are presented as simply and clearly as possible and can be put to use in one's daily life. I hope, therefore, to make it readable but not simplistic.

That being said, I must admit that this book was not an easy one to write. I had to sit with the questions ruminating in my heart sometimes for a long time, and, as strange as this may seem, I actually found myself praying through some topics—being "in" them rather than thinking through them. It is my hope that the reader will allow this to take place in her or his encounter with the reflections offered here as well. Words from Bernadette Farrell's musical adaptation of Psalm 139 keep repeating themselves within me as I write this: "With love everlasting you besiege me," and "You are with me beyond my understanding: God of my present, my past and future, too."[2] I believe that the mystical dimensions in the thoughts of Meister Eckhart, of Teilhard de Chardin, of the integrative philosopher Ken Wilber, of systems thinker Ervin Laszlo, of exegetes, theologians, and others that are reflected on in these pages need to be prayed through slowly, and patiently lived into. A "quick read" will very likely not prove very satisfying or helpful.

Sources for deeper research and further exploration will, as in all my other books, be indicated in the notes. Because I have been engaged with the task of "faith seeking understanding" in many of my prior writings, the reader will find here a continuity and expansion of topics addressed especially in my last three books: *On Becoming Who We Are: Passionate Musings in the Winter of Life* (2012); *Awe-Filled Wonder: The Interface of Science and Spirituality* (2008); and *From Religion Back to Faith: A Journey of the Heart* (2006).

My gratitude goes first and foremost to the many scholars whose writings have given the inspiration and impetus for this book. Their help will be duly acknowledged throughout these pages. To my friends, once again, and to my Community for their interest, encouragement, and support, my heartfelt thanks. Thank you especially to S. Joyce Hoben, SND, for her editorial advice. My deep appreciation goes also to the composer and singer Carolyn McDade for permission to use the title of one of her truly inspiring songs as the title of this book. To those who have gone before me into the Mystery of Love that awaits us all, and who continue to encourage and help me through dreams and unexpected insights, I thank you and I love you always. Special among these are Clare Gebhardt, SND, who always nudged me to express exactly but kindly what I thought; the "Padre," Leon Lajoie, S.J., for being there—always a friend in need; and finally, my parents, who ever encouraged my questioning and probing. My thanks go also to my publisher for the kind support and encouragement, and to the patient editors who worked with me so faithfully.

Thoughts and Questions for Meditation

1. How do you relate to the observation and discussion of the first few pages regarding our nature as "planetary people, pilgrim people whose ecstasy is in the journey"?

2. Do you agree with the following: Authentic maturation for individuals, cultures, as well as religions, inevitably makes demands on all of us. The "living waters" of faith cannot be static forever without growing stale. "Drinking" into their depths demands a constant transformation of our understanding.

3. How do you understand the description of truth as "an evolving relationship between the knower and what *reveals itself* to her or him" based on the fact that human beings can grasp their reality only according to their intellectual and cultural capacity at any time of their development?

4. What is your reaction to the "disturbing questions" raised in the Reflection section of this chapter?

2

For Unto Us a Child Is Born, a Son Is Given (Isaiah 9:6)

There was a man who lived some two thousand or so years ago. He was proclaimed Son of God, Redeemer, Lord, Savior of the world, Liberator, who brought peace to humankind. He was God made manifest. His birth was extraordinary. He was born of a woman overshadowed and impregnated by God, hence he was God from God. His birth marked the beginning of a new era—even a new calendar. His story was glad tidings (*euaggelion*—gospel, good news). He brought down the mighty from their thrones. Who was this man?

Much to the surprise of most Christians today, this man was, in fact, proclaimed to be Caesar Augustus, adopted son of Julius Caesar, and first emperor of Rome from 27 BCE to 14 CE. His earthly mother was Atia, married to Gaius Octavius, who, it was said, in a dream some time before Augustus was born saw the sun rise from Atia's womb. She also "dreamed that her vitals were borne up to the stars and spread over the whole extent of land and sea."[1]

The account presented above belongs to Roman imperial theology in the centuries before and after the birth of Jesus. It shocked me the first time I learned of this, because, like most Christians, I had believed that what was there claimed for Caesar Augustus belonged to no one except Jesus. For years I had recited both the Nicene and the Apostles' creeds that seemed to affirm my belief:

> I believe in one Lord Jesus Christ, the only Begotten
> Son of God, . . . God from God, Light from Light, true
> God from true God, begotten, not made, one in being
> with the Father; through Him all things were made . . .
> *for our salvation* . . . by the Holy Spirit was incarnate
> of the Virgin Mary . . . his kingdom will have no end.
> (Nicene Creed)

The Apostles' Creed is shorter and has fewer similarities but
depicts him nevertheless as Son of God:

> I believe in God, the Father almighty, and in Jesus
> Christ, his only Son, our Lord, who was conceived by
> the Holy Spirit, born of the Virgin Mary.

A Story Born of Hope

Years before these creeds were written, Paul certainly, and
the evangelists after him, spoke of Jesus in a similar manner.
What I did not know, and what is not often taught except
in more advanced theology courses, is that in writing about
Jesus as Son of God and thus placing him on an equal foot-
ing with the emperor and lord of Roman society, the early
Christian writers dared to challenge its oppressive power
structure. The scriptural accounts, especially their claims
concerning the divinity of Jesus, were in Roman times a cou-
rageous call for transformation aimed at moving away from
the apparent peace and order achieved through the domination and violence that were the rule of *pax Romana,* and
advocating the *nonviolent* peace of Jesus Christ and of the
God he proclaimed. Theirs was a story born of hope for a
new vision and of a life centered in God. The metaphors they
used in exalting Jesus, of who he was and how he was conceived, were clearly those of their time and not only paralleled but actually exceeded those used for Caesar Augustus.[2]

In that way they very likely intended to point to Jesus not only as a voice in opposition to Roman domination but as a challenge to the entire Roman imperial ideology.

Even though Matthew and Luke, for example, present very different narratives dealing with the birth of Jesus, they both claim for him an extraordinary conception in the Virgin Mary by the power of the Holy Spirit "overshadowing" her. They proclaim him as the Son God, as savior, Messiah, king, and ruler whose reign would have no end. Furthermore, the claim of divine sonship for Jesus by virtue of his birth is in these Gospels enhanced by their accounts of his baptism. There God is said to claim Jesus as God's Son in a manner generally understood to indicate adoption, or sonship by election. This practice was recognized and accepted in the Roman culture of the first two centuries when even slaves could be elevated through adoption by the *pater familias*, and in this way could earn the right to succession.[3] Caesar Augustus himself was the adopted son of (the divine) Julius Caesar, and claimed the right of succession because of that. His eventual stature and glory were, of course, enhanced further by the belief that he was also begotten of God.

In narrating the event of Jesus's baptism, where a voice from heaven declares that Jesus is God's ("my") Son—the beloved with whom God is ("I am") well pleased, Mark, who begins his Gospel that way and, contrary to Matthew and Luke, has no birth narrative, also uses the adoption metaphor in order to claim Jesus as the Son of God and to indicate God's very clear design on him. John also uses the adoption narrative, although with some slight variation. In his Gospel, John the Baptist relates the event, claiming that he had seen the Spirit descend on Jesus in the form of a dove and that it was communicated to him that Jesus indeed was the Son of God. John, however, strengthens the claim regarding the divinity of Jesus by the prologue to his Gospel, where he attributes divine preexistence to Jesus as the Word who was with God from the beginning.

Claiming for Jesus of Nazareth, the itinerant preacher from Nazareth in Galilee, the glory and status that were at that time unquestionably attributed and reserved to the emperor of Rome was clearly an extraordinary and daring undertaking. It was a statement about the presence of God and about where God had chosen to reveal God's self. It moved divine self-revelation from the glories of imperial power to a peasant—whom some would have regarded as a nobody. It was an insult, a heresy, and it was treason. As Dominic Crossan points out:

> Christians were not simply using ordinary titles applied to all sorts of people at that time, or even extraordinary titles applied to special people in the East. They were taking the identity of the Roman emperor and giving it to a Jewish peasant. Either that was a peculiar joke and a very low lampoon, or it was what the Romans called *majesta* and we call high treason.[4]

It would seem then that for Paul and for the other Christian missionaries of his day, as well as for the evangelists who came some years later, the symbols and metaphors they used when speaking about Jesus were not merely instructions, information about how, over the years after the resurrection, they had come to understand who Jesus of Nazareth was and what he had taught. Their declarations were also symbolic of a counter-movement to Roman imperial theology. They claimed that Jesus was *their* Lord, *not* Caesar. Jesus was to be followed, *not* the emperor. His peace was the true way of salvation, *not* the *pax Romana*. Once again, Dominic Crossan puts it well when he identifies the peace of Christ simply as "religion, nonviolence, justice, peace," in contrast to the "peace of Rome," won through war, victory, and, only after that, a peace that was always and at best tenuous— ever requiring further violence whenever resistance to the "victor" reared its head.[5]

The Emergence of God in Human Form

Before we move on and probe more directly into our response to the deeper meaning of a Christian "counter-movement" to the wars and violence of today, and to the shameful "peace" of any "imperial theology," there is one question we may still need to ask regarding some of the metaphors used in Christian scripture during the time of the evangelists. How might we understand them today and for our times? It would seem to me that those who only now have become aware of the claims to divinity by Caesar Augustus and his follow- ers could quite easily be tempted to relegate such claims to ancient mythology and primitive religion. Certainly the snake through which Apollo impregnated Atia lacks enough sophistication to fit into that category. But even ignoring that, what *did* people mean when they blithely attributed divine sonship to a mere mortal? Furthermore, could it not also be suggested, no matter how uncomfortably, that if the claim to divinity for Augustus is mere mythology, this would also have to be true in the case of Jesus?

A question such as this can clearly be unnerving for Chris- tians in the light of the creeds recited and the dogmas that have been declared around this question. Few of us, I sug- gest, feel at ease even mentioning it. But does not an hon- est quest into what it is we *believe* and what we *mean* by the symbols and metaphors we use demand that we address this concern? Perhaps we could start by quite simply asking ourselves whether it would be possible for us still to believe in the Divine fully present and acting in and through Jesus if we were temporarily to put aside all of the literature con- cerning Mary's virginal conception and all the declarations concerning the divine sonship of Jesus based on that event. I firmly believe that it would be possible, and that this belief, *deeply reflected on*, would also enhance our understanding of his humanity, as well as ours. This is the task, as I see it, of this book. It is the task of Christian faith truly "seeking understanding" at this time in the evolution of human consciousness.

It seems obvious enough that the act of human procreation when applied to God needs to be understood as a metaphor. It is an attempt to say something symbolically that cannot easily be spoken in regular human discourse. As I have mentioned in a number of my other writings, metaphors contain within themselves both a negation (a "no") and an affirmation (a "yes"). The former, in reference to the question under discussion, would today certainly apply to "physical procreation" as a way of understanding the fatherhood of God. Scripture claims that Jesus encouraged us to call God *our* "Father." Clearly, none of us would understand this as referring to our biological origins. Also, when we read that Jesus claimed that he and the Father are one (John 10:30), would it not seem strange were we to interpret this statement as a claim to physical procreation? The God we believe in is Spirit and does not have a gender even if some Christians find this difficult to accept. Physicality as such does not belong to the spiritual world. The use of symbols, therefore, such as "father" or "mother," such as "walking among us," "embracing us," or "seeing" what we do might be more meaningfully understood as articulating a depth *experience* of relatedness, of love; a sense of well being, of security and presence, rather than a physical reality. Our faith sees God as creator, source of everything that is. The metaphors we use are attempts at understanding the mystery of this.

What then can we affirm when we use a parental metaphor for God's relation to Jesus? The careful phrasing Roger Haight uses in his powerful study *Jesus Symbol of God* seems to me one of the most meaningful approaches to this question: "It is no less than God with whom we are confronted in Jesus."[6] This is a profound faith statement by which we hold that the Holy One, the source of everything that is, emerged most fully in Jesus of Nazareth. We hold that in everything Jesus stood for, lived, and proclaimed, he was and still is the clearest expression of God's presence in our midst. Our faith proclaims God as the source of the perfection, goodness, compassion, mercy, and love manifest in Jesus. The divine in him graced and sanctified his humanity; allowed it to be suffused by and to manifest *no less than God*. And as amazing as this is, there is still more, for even as Jesus embodied divinity in his humanity, *he challenges us to follow him*. He articulated this experience in terms of being the "child" of God and urged us to believe this of ourselves as well. For me this invitation is the most meaningful and empowering aspect of this reflection. As I mentioned in *Awe Filled Wonder*,

> Taking in the power of this insight (something, I believe, that can happen only slowly and with deliberate attention) brings to our awareness that we, since we are human too, are therefore also called to this emergence, called to the truth and integrity and holiness of our humanity. The life of Jesus was the "presencing" of God. Ours is called to be that as well, as we embrace the fullness of our humanity and walk into the Christ story that becomes paradigmatic, a saving grace for all of us.[7]

Our Journey into Depth

It is quite certain, of course, that what we have come to embrace as the substance of the Christian faith was not something that was claimed by the followers of Jesus on their first encounter with him or even during their subsequent time spent with him. His life and message had an extraordinary impact on those who followed him, to be sure, but like all depth experiences it needed time, in fact many years, to be more deeply understood, acknowledged, assimilated, and interpreted, especially after his death and what his followers experienced as his resurrection. Edward Schillebeeckx says this well:

To begin with, perhaps, [interpretation] is still implicit, and only later is it brought to the level of reflection. The renewal of life which Jesus had evoked from his disciples and the process he had started off led the disciples to reflect on their experience. They began to analyze it, to consider its various aspects and give it a place in their consciousness. . . . Familiar things became familiar in a new way, now that the followers of Jesus had a new focal point. On the basis of their common experience they arrived at what we might call a Christian theory of grace, . . . a thematic account of the meaning of Christian redemption and Christian salvation. . . . Every single New Testament writing, every gospel and every epistle, is concerned with the salvation experienced in and through Jesus.[8]

Schillebeeckx called the study from which this citation is taken *Christ.* This was the title given to Jesus in the light of the resurrection experience and in conjunction with the eventual movement of evangelization beyond Palestine into the Greco-Roman gentile world. It referred to him as "the Lord's anointed," fulfilling the Messianic prophecy. It was not claimed by Jesus himself but eventually was connected to his very name (Jesus Christ). It also became the hallmark of those who believed in him and what he stood for (Christians), and who formed community (Christianity) around living and proclaiming that vision.

Reflection

As I am writing this, I am wondering what the declaration that "Jesus is the Christ" means for us today. Christianity, if it is *truly* embraced and lived, is an extraordinary challenge! Paul, as well as the other missionaries of his day, took that challenge, and they died for their convictions, as did *their* Lord and *ours.* It seems to me that a religion that puts its primary emphasis merely on unquestioning "acceptance" of propositions about theological content and faithful obedience to those who declare them is easy in comparison. But, as I mentioned already, those who first proclaimed Jesus as their Lord were not primarily content oriented. Jesus, after all, did not write a single dictum or rule. His and his early followers' concerns were with action and with transformation. The disciples spoke of their experience and proclaimed Christ's vision with their lives. That is why they were ready to suffer for it. *Are we?* Or has our faith, and has the faith of the church to which we belong, become too comfortable? Has it "morphed" perhaps into just another one of a number of religions that propose diverse theories about the Source of our existence? Sometimes these theories can be all absorbing, and their followers then can become excited about believing them as the only true ones; about debating, arguing with, and even condemning those who are excited about other theories. But most of the time and sadly, merely *having* that kind of religion can be just *that,* and not much more.

Several years ago in the United States, the Leadership Conference of Women Religious (LCWR) drew the ire of their bishops for their alleged lack of support (their silence—that up to now has always been interpreted as consent) regarding the bishops' opposition to the proposed national Affordable (health) Care Act. It seems that the women's primary concern and deep involvement with matters of social justice, but their silence regarding perceived immoral regulations in the health-care proposal (i.e., its ruling regarding contraception), proved disturbing to the prelates. The Conference therefore was subjected to a lengthy, humiliating, and tedious examination and supervision ordered by Rome's Congregation for the Doctrine of the Faith (CDF). This ostensibly was to make sure that they and their policies were doctrinally on target, and that they would not allow themselves to listen to anyone who might have thoughts dangerous to Catholic teaching.

"Thought control" such as this seems to me not only anachronistic but also deeply offensive. The reaction, in the form of outrage, by Catholics in the United States and even worldwide was a clear indication that they concur. It is my sense that they, as do I, believe that the *living waters* that flow through our hearts and empower our faith "sing" of a different approach and a different vision. *That* vision is not primarily concerned with intellectual exercises, moral and doctrinal propositions, and the absolutes flowing from them. It rejects paternalistic supervision, dogmatism, high-handedness and domination of any kind, no matter what "holy" declarations are made in their defense.[9]

A Child Is Born

The concern of this book is faith seeking understanding in our time. This faith, as I keep stressing, is primarily centered on the person of Jesus and the Good News about God's desire for us that he preached and modeled by his life. The first followers of Jesus used parables and metaphors to teach what he was about. It would seem that their concern was not primarily exact historical data, although clearly some of that is present in their accounts. They wrote in the parabolic style of their time and culture to reach those familiar with that approach, to touch their hearts and invite transformation. Perhaps they may also have found that parables and metaphors were the only possible way to speak and write meaningfully about Jesus and what he stood for, since neither he, nor his message about God, could possibly be contained in the dry language of moralism or the turgid expositions of laws and propositions.

The Christmas stories of Matthew and Luke illustrate this well. As I mentioned earlier, only Matthew and Luke tell us about the birth of Jesus. However, except for the fact that both claim that Jesus—the "Son of David"—was born in Bethlehem, their story lines are totally different. In spite of this, they have been merged over the years in such a way that Christians now generally see them as one story and celebrate them as such. Unfortunately for those attached to a historical interpretation of scripture stories, exegetes point out that their fundamental differences would indicate that they very likely are not factual. Exegesis identifies multiple and independent attestations of the same account as one indication of its historical authenticity. The fact that there are none of these that we are aware of addressing the birth of Jesus would suggest that no one really knew much about him until he began his public ministry.

Factual certainty, of course, is not the only criterion for truth. It is necessary in courts of law, but on a deeper level something can be true without being factual. The story that Jesus told about the Good Samaritan, for example, was clearly a parable, and therefore its factual nature is irrelevant. By that is meant that it does not matter whether there actually was a Good Samaritan who did what the story relates. The story is nonetheless deeply true in an exemplary way when it is viewed as an answer to the question "Who then is my neighbor?" Its exemplary truth-value has been recognized multiple times by those who have received or shown unsolicited kindness and generosity in situations of need. Perhaps the same is true of the parables about the birth of Jesus and what it means for our salvation. Our concern then needs to be with the truth-value of these stories, not so much with their historical accuracy. Since they are very likely not historical, we need to ask ourselves why they were written in the first place, and how, or in what way, they are true.

During the retreats and workshops I give, especially around the Advent season, I usually tell the participants that Christmas and what it teaches us is *big time* and that it may perhaps be *the* most important feast for Christianity. Now, we know that generally this honor is given to the feast of the resurrection and clearly who can argue that? But we also know that there would not have been an Easter if there had not first been a birth and a life. To divert for a moment from his birth to his life, I have often wondered, particularly as I grew older, why this has been so totally ignored in both the Nicene and the Apostles' creeds. These creeds are our profession of faith. They address what we believe Jesus was about. Yet in their declarations they both move immediately from his birth to his suffering, his death, and then to the resurrection. But, was not his *life* and its *message* the reason for his persecution, his execution, and ultimately for his vindication by God? The presence of Christ Jesus in our midst and what he showed us about God's vision for us is the primary inspiration for authentic and lived faith. That, I believe, is why ignoring it in our creeds can have dire consequences.

The parables of the birth of Christ, when reflected on beyond the tinsel and the bells that we have superimposed on them, are in fact an amazing foreshadowing of what the concerns of his life would be about and what his God wants us to care about as well. Sadly, our celebrations of Christmas, as lovely as they may be, have in many ways obscured the gospel message. What these celebrations can easily blind us to is that Christ's birth and its story are meant to be *our* story. It was told that we might take it in and learn from it. Christmas, above all else, invites us to meditate and internalize who the God of Jesus really is, what this God is about, and who this God is for. It invites us to embrace this reality, to walk into it, and to make it our own. Dietrich Bonhoeffer says it well:

> If God . . . wants to come into this world in the manger at Bethlehem, that is no idyllic family affair, but the beginning of a complete turnaround, a reordering of everything on this earth. If we wish to take part in this Advent and Christmas event, then we cannot simply be bystanders or onlookers, as if we were at the theater, enjoying all the cheerful images. No, we ourselves are swept up into the action there, into this conversion of all things. . . . We cannot withdraw.[10]

Our God, so Luke's story tells us, is a God who chose to take on the human condition in utter destitution—as a poor child, born of poor parents who did not have enough money even to pay for shelter in an inn so that their child could be safely born. (I actually wonder whether Luke by telling us this story really meant that there was in fact no room in the inn. My own perhaps more cynical take is that the manager of the inn might not have wanted to be bothered with the trouble of admitting a poor man with a fully pregnant wife ready to give birth in his facility, and that he turned them away with the convenient excuse of "no room.") In either case, the story tells us that the God who, we believe, emerged in our midst as a little innocent baby boy was born in an open courtyard, where the animals belonging to the inn were kept. There he was "laid in one of their feeding troughs."[11] I suspect that the place was dirty and cold—no golden bells, red poinsettias, and sweet-smelling straw. Joseph very likely was deeply ashamed, and Mary, very tired, scared, discouraged, and in pain. Luke also tells us that the presence of God, as manifest in the baby Jesus, was not announced to the mighty—the city magistrates or leaders of the synagogues. Angelic messengers came to the lowly and the poor, the marginalized—shepherds who really were the rejects of society at that time. Heavenly messengers spoke to *them* about his birth, not to the powerful and influential of the time.

As our merged Christmas story continues in Matthew, we are told that God, *as revealed in Jesus*, shortly after he was born *welcomed* "foreigners," the Magi, (we also call them "wise men"). Matthew portrays them as having traveled from afar, and as eager to meet Jesus, whom Matthew depicts in this way as savior, not only of the Jewish people but also of gentiles. "Those [also] are 'his people' whom he will 'save from their sins'" (1:21).[12] Matthew also tells us that, shortly after the wise men depart, Jesus and his parents become refugees. They have to flee from those who do not want the reign Jesus has come to proclaim, the salvation from oppression and domination. Right from the beginning, therefore, the God revealed in Jesus faces the powers of darkness. Ultimately, crucified as a common criminal and rejected by those in power, God in Jesus endures the dregs of the human condition, *but loves us still.*

If we believe that Christianity is really about the emergence of God in time and space, about God's becoming present in our very midst; if we claim this belief as a recognized, acknowledged, and celebrated reality, then this has to be our primary message. It is a message we proclaim by our words and deeds; a message we *live.* God so loved us as to make us part of the extraordinary event of divine self-revelation in love and compassion throughout creation! God took on *our* human form, became one with *us.* This is the deep truth that energizes our faith and gives it meaning. It is the truth that cannot simply be talked about and preached from pulpits, but must be lived and proclaimed *by our lives.* But is this in fact our reality? Do we truly embrace it and live it?

The symbols of the Christmas parables jolt us into some serious self-examination. They move us beyond the doctrinal emphasis on "two natures in one person," on "begotten, not made," on "consubstantial," on "divine sonship," important as they may be. They expose us, instead, to the passion and faithfulness of a God who so loved us as to enter into the human condition of weakness and betrayal, of the will to power and obsession with violence, only to redeem us ultimately, and to draw us back into the unending mercy and compassion that is divine love.

To summarize, then:

- The stories of Christ's birth tell of how God emerged in a baby lying in a trough where animals were meant to eat, because humanity had no room for the Divine in human form. *Is this our story still?*
- They speak of how those who claimed that they were waiting for Emmanuel could not see the holy presence

among them, did not appreciate the gift that was offered them, and were oblivious of the light that foreigners recognized and came to worship. *Are we as blind as they were?*

- They point to how those obsessed with their own power and privilege saw in his coming only defeat and eventual ruin for themselves, and allowed fear to drive them to violence. *Is this true of today's society as well?*
- Of course shepherds and foreigners too, and the lowly and rejected ones, heard the message of God's love and rejoiced. *What do we have to see and to accept of God's message in order to be able truly to rejoice with them?*

What is the lived reality of our Christian faith today? I wonder at times whether perhaps in the doctrines and official belief systems of our religion the excessive emphasis on the divinity of Jesus might not serve as an excuse not to pay enough attention to his life among us in human form. Might it be blinding us from the necessity of entering his story lived for *our* living? God in Jesus was born and lived *among* us, not *above* us. What the Christmas stories symbolize for us is that not recognizing and acknowledging this presence in our midst blinds us to the essence of what humanity is called to be and to become. In many ways the Christmas symbols are tragic reminders of what can happen when we ignore our own intrinsic potential for goodness, for mercy and compassion. God in Christ lived among us to show us that and in this way somehow, strange and miraculous as this may seem, offers us the opportunity to acknowledge our own potential for divinization.

Thoughts and Questions for Meditation

1. What is your reaction to Roman imperial theology and its similarity to the proclamations made about Jesus and his birth?

2. How do you relate to the adoption narratives in the Gospels and the mixed metaphors in both Matthew and Luke? What deeper message can one draw from this seeming contradiction about the divinity of Jesus? What do you think people of ancient times meant when they blithely attributed divine sonship to a mere mortal?

3. John Dominic Crossan compares the Peace of Christ and the *pax Romana*. Which one seems prominent in today's world?

4. What is your reaction to Schillebeeckx's reflection on the gradual development of Christology?

5. Do you agree that Christianity is a tough religion that is not primarily content but rather action oriented. Is this your experience of your faith?

6. What does the "depth" interpretation of the Christmas story tell you about the God of Jesus? I am referring specifically to the last paragraph of this chapter.

3

My Soul Rejoices

My being proclaims your greatness,
and my spirit finds joy in you, God my Savior.
For you looked upon me, your servant, in my lowli-
    ness;
all ages to come shall call me blessed.
God, you who are mighty, have done great things
    for me.
Holy is your name.
Your mercy is from age to age toward those who
    fear you.
You have shown might with your arm
and confused the proud in their inmost thoughts.
You have deposed the mighty from their thrones
and raised the lowly to high places.
The hungry you have given every good thing
while the rich you have sent away empty.
You have upheld Israel your servant, ever mindful of
    your mercy—
even as you promised our ancestors;
promised Abraham, Sarah, and their descendants
    forever.[1]

A Woman's Passion Ignored

In his Advent reflections, preached in 1933, Dietrich Bonhoeffer—then a pastor in London—calls Mary's Magnificat

> . . . at once the most passionate, the wildest, and one
> might even say, the most revolutionary Advent hymn
> ever sung. This is not the gentle, tender, dreamy Mary
> whom we sometimes see in paintings; this is the pas-
> sionate, surrendered, proud, enthusiastic Mary who
> speaks out here. This song has none of the sweet, nos-
> talgic, or even playful tones of some of our Christmas
> carols. It is, instead, a hard, strong, inexorable song
> about collapsing thrones and humbled lords of this
> world, about the power of God and the powerless-
> ness of humankind. These are the tones of the women
> prophets of the Old Testament that now come to life
> in Mary's mouth.[2]

Bonhoeffer's reflection fills me with deep awe of a woman
about whom we really know very little as far as the Christian scriptures are concerned. Paul never mentions her by
name, saying only that "God sent forth his son born of a
woman" (Galatians 4:4). This statement may sound strange
today. How else would anyone be born? Paul's emphasis,
however, was on the true humanity of Jesus who, he points
out, was born the way of all humans. The Synoptic Gospels
mention her in the beginning with reference to the birth of
Jesus (Luke and Matthew), once in his childhood when he
remained behind in the Temple (Luke). There are some references to her, together with his siblings, during the public
life of Jesus (the Synoptic Gospels). John mentions her at a
wedding in the beginning of Jesus' public life and with the
disciple John at the foot of the cross. In the Acts of the Apostles, Luke mentions her only once, when he comments on
the events after the ascension experience. She, the apostles,

and the brothers of Jesus are said to have returned to Jerusalem and, together with some other women, to have devoted themselves to constant prayer.

Mark, the writer of the first Gospel, does not always write kindly about Mary, implying a certain lack of understanding about Jesus's mission on her part. Luke's writings, on the other hand, are more positive. Because these events are usually not multiply and independently attested, we have very little reliable scriptural data for her.

Mary's ascendency in Christianity's movement toward self-understanding seems slow but took on momentum as the centuries progressed. During the first two centuries references to her are rare. The emphasis in the early church, particularly in the second century, seems to have been on the historical reality of Mary's virginity and on her virginal conception in particular. My sense is that today this is of little interest to most Christians even if Catholics keep reciting it in their creeds. Though there was dissent around this topic in the early years of Christianity, the majority of ancient references seem to have been in agreement. References to the miraculous birth of Jesus (i.e., Mary remaining a virgin while giving birth) date to around the second century.

The belief in Mary's *perpetual* virginity, however, arose sometime later. I find it somewhat puzzling, since it seems to contradict the Gospels' multiple references to Jesus's brothers and sisters. By the third century, however, when consecrated virginity had been established as a special state in the church and Mary was held up as the perfect model for those aspiring to this state, her perpetual virginity had been accepted by most of the Church Fathers, both Latin and Greek. In fact she was hailed as the model of all virtues. Richard P. McBrien, in his extensive study *Catholicism,* to which I am indebted for much of this historical information, offers an interesting aside concerning "the outstanding exception" to the early veneration of Mary, John Chrysostom, who apparently had little good to say about the Mother of Jesus and her support of him. Two of his remarks cited by McBrien illustrate this well. Both are made in homilies on John's Gospel: "She did not cease to think little of (Jesus) . . . but herself she thought everywhere worthy of the fist place, because she was his mother." About her request of Jesus at the wedding in Cana, Chrysostom comments, "She wanted to confer a favor on others, and render herself more illustrious through her Son."[3] Since Chrysostom seems to have had problems with women generally,[4] his observations about Mary do not seem too surprising. Like most of the negative comments about women by him and other early Church Fathers, these statements are sad but would not be terribly relevant for us today except for the fact that these observations (made in another age and cultural setting), even if they are not consciously acknowledged or even remembered in our time, still seem to influence church policies regarding women to this very day.

Questions for Our Time

Who then is Mary for us today? I have struggled with this question for some time now and do not feel that Marian devotions and attitudes toward her in our official church are of much help in answering this question. For one, as I mentioned already, the emphasis on Mary's virginity (before, but especially during and after the birth of Jesus) does not seem important to people today and certainly not to the women I know. Why is sexual abstinence still claimed to be so sacred by our ecclesial establishment? Are our bodies diminished by physical love? If two persons truly love each other, why should the expression of that love not embrace the totality of their being, including their physicality? Why should any aspect of God's creation be considered inferior to any other, be vilified, or belittled?

We are spirited bodies who were intended this way by our creator. As such we are whole, and every part and dimension of our being is holy. Some of us abstain from the sexual expression of our love, not because it is inferior or evil, but because the love we are being called to may demand a commitment to the many rather than the singular gift of ourselves to a significant other. The intensity of sexual union, together with the responsibilities that flow from this expression of love, is by its very nature focused. Because of the fidelity it requires, other love priorities need to be subordinated to one's covenantal commitments and obligations. Regarding virginity (celibacy) and its relevance today, I refer the reader to two of my previous books where I have written at length about the vow of celibacy as an expression of virginal love and of its place in our human quest for the Holy.[5] Suffice it to say here that I see it as complementary to, not as holier than, marriage. It is a different call, *not* a "superior" one.

Both calls when lived with integrity speak to the sacredness of human loving and its expression of the divine energy coursing through all of creation. The continued reference to a life of virginity as being "a consecrated life" can therefore be rather confusing because of what it has come to imply: Words such as *sacred, hallowed, blessed, being set apart* are all synonyms for the "consecrated" life. They can easily imply an unwarranted separation from the "ordinary," pointing to a "higher state of perfection" that in the past was associated with bridal mysticism, that is, seeing the virgin as a "bride of Christ." It is, at best, a puzzling metaphor in today's world, a vestige of the long history of Christianity's fascination with a dualistic divide between soul (spirit) and body (matter). It claimed superiority for soul or spirit and rejected the body and its pleasures.[6]

We are created as we are: holy and intended to be whole. Every walk in life is meant to be a sacred journey into the depths of our humanity where alone God can be found. Terms such as "higher" and "lower," therefore, when referencing our way of being are unwarranted, divisive, and debilitating. In the light of what today's holistic spirituality has come to understand and insist on regarding the holiness of all creation, it would seem that an excessive concern with the virginity of the Mother of Jesus—as a sign of greater sanctity and specialness—is no longer helpful. It is the *entire* Mary— passionate, surrendered, proud, enthusiastic, as Bonhoeffer describes her, to whom we need to pay attention. She it is who points us to the "collapsing thrones and humbled lords of this world," to "the power of God and the powerlessness of humankind," that the Christmas story we reflected on earlier announces. Whether she does this as a virgin or not is a question that can only distract and therefore seems irrelevant to me.

Mary of Nazareth, Mother of Jesus

For our imitation, therefore, the full and uncompromised humanity of Mary is extremely important. Her motherhood was real, with all its joys and sorrows. If indeed she knew from the beginning about the specialness of her son (a question that can be answered in the affirmative only by faith), she could not have known the pain she would endure in witnessing his betrayal and his ultimate agony and death. Contrary to what is intimated in the Gospel of Mark, I believe that as someone who reared Jesus, Mary would have had to be deeply aware of his passion for God's reign. She would have felt his eagerness to bear witness to the compassion and tenderness of the God whom he saw *for all of us* as Abba. Mary would have known the hurt at the misunderstanding and rejection Jesus experienced, and she would have felt them most keenly with him. Mothers know these things and endure them with their children.

As a woman, I am drawn most deeply to Mary when I reflect on the mother "beneath" the cross.[7] The deep truth of this story touches for me most profoundly who Mary was— the Sorrowful Mother. Her perpetual virginity, as interesting as this may have been for the Fathers of the Church, says little to most women in today's world. But in a world torn once again by war and brutality, by the dregs of poverty, hunger, and homelessness, the mother beneath the cross speaks of solidarity, of understanding, of presence and compassion. She is not the woman in blue standing on a distant pedestal high over some altar. She is flesh and blood, caring and true. Admiration and veneration can be discouraging, especially if what is looked up to is impossible to reach. Perpetual virginity, especially during the birth process, is certainly that. It is astounding and impossible to fathom, but what else can it possibly be? The woman "beneath" the cross is Mother to us all. No one matures without at least some pain and suffering. They are part of the human story that invites us into depth, and Mary knows this and finds us there.

And yet there is still more. Even as I reflect on what I have just written, it occurs to me that in order to gain a more complete appreciation of what Mary can mean to us in contemporary times we might need to consider also the beginning. By this I mean Mary's actual *experience* of mothering Jesus from the start. This is something often overlooked and therefore neglected, since it is a reality that only women can know. It too needs to be freed, I believe, from a subtle depreciation of Mary that, unintentionally perhaps (or not), has been ignored in earlier and less "woman conscious" times. I find it interesting, for example, that even in our Advent devotions Mary's actual pregnancy—*the most intimate time for mother and child*—is virtually ignored. We pray for the "coming" of the Messiah, when, in fact, he is already there *in her body* and, therefore, *with us* on this earth. No one knows this better than his Mother and any other woman who has ever been pregnant, who has fed her child from within her body and given of her blood for its survival. But how could a church where for centuries women were not allowed to speak publicly in any setting—certainly not about their intimate experiences—and where they were barred from studying theology even into the twentieth century possibly know this?

For many years I used to celebrate Advent by placing a statue of a pregnant woman in the center of my Advent

wreath. I also sent homemade Christmas cards of pho-
tographs depicting Mother and Child with the following
inscription: "And Woman said: This is my Body. This is my
Blood."[8] The reality of this statement and its implications are
obvious to those who have eyes to see and hearts to "hear"
beyond the "but it has never been done." Mary provided not
only the tabernacle as housing for the Divine, but in fact gave
of her own body and blood to the God made flesh in Jesus.
It seems to me that the priesthood of Mary has been ignored
even to this day, largely because of our fear to contextualize our beliefs, to "drink 'deep'" and truly to wade into the
"living waters" of our time. Instead we seem obsessed with
past erroneous theories, perceptions, and loyalties. However
we may want to understand the importance and necessity of
male procreative activity, for example, we know today that
it would in fact go nowhere without a woman's gift of her
embodiment. What has been unknown or ignored in the past
is taught today in any elementary anatomy class. If for no
other reason than intellectual honesty, Catholicism, in particular, needs to acknowledge that Mary's womb is "blessed"
not merely because it carried Jesus and provided a temporary
place for him but because it generated his very body and
blood. If we could see that, we would at least recognize that
her role in bringing about God's presence among us through
Jesus was more than a simple and obedient but passive *"be it
done unto me,"* as important as this was.

I believe, furthermore, that the mother of Jesus shared
with him not only her flesh and her blood. She shared with
him her wisdom as well, and her tender love. The song that
sprang from her heart when she became aware of her pregnancy was exultation in the face of God's mystery and power.
"The tones [and wisdom] of the women prophets of the Old
Testament came to life in Mary's mouth," Bonhoeffer insists.
It seems impossible for me to believe that they would not
have become a part of her life and were not passed on to
her child. They also strengthened her in the face of certainly

the greatest pain a mother can ever endure—witnessing the execution of her son.

The Mystical Aspect of Virgin Motherhood

The Christ's Breath

I am a hole in a flute
That the Christ's breath moves through—
Listen to this music.

Hafiz (c. 1320–1389)

The virginity of Mary as discussed in the above sections of this chapter (especially with reference to "during and after" the birth of Jesus) has in our tradition suffered from what I believe to be a culturally conditioned insistence on the factual as well as on its superiority. As such, it has become largely incomprehensible for us today, alienating us from a treasured icon of our faith. The mystical and symbolic approach to the power and significance of "virgin motherhood" has in past centuries, however, been meaningful to many and, I believe, could be that for our time as well. I have, in a number of my earlier books,[9] reflected extensively not so much on Mary as Virgin Mother (although the Christian concept surely originates with her) but on a mystical call for all of us, women and men alike, to embrace the deep meaning of this symbol and to live into it. To avoid unnecessary duplication with my previous writings, therefore, I will here simply try to highlight the most important aspects of this mystical call. I feel the need to do so not only for the sake of completeness but also in order to honor the profound mystical tradition that has paralleled so many approaches to this powerful symbol that in our time have become less meaningful.

For the great Dominican preacher and mystic Meister Eckhart (c. 1260–1327/29) the deep meaning of virginity points quite simply to emptiness waiting to be filled. With respect to giving life, the virgin waiting to be mother symbolizes expectancy, readiness, as well as a potential to receive and bear fruit. But what does this mean in the spiritual realm? For Eckhart, our openness to God and to God's creation finds its most authentic expression in an attitude of receptive responsiveness—an attitude that is free enough, "empty" enough, to let God be God in our life and in all of creation. He urges us to recognize the Divine there, to refrain from limiting, categorizing, and defining who and where God is; to allow the different, the strange and foreign we encounter in other cultures, religions, and persons to be what it is and to honor it as such. The German word for this, *Gelassenheit* (often translated as "releasement"[10] and implying the attitude of being released, being set free in order to let be), is most accurately understood as a readiness to do precisely that. One refrains from imposing judgment, from trying to create others in one's own likeness, from allowing one's own assumptions, presuppositions, and prejudices to dominate one's approach to the other. One is empty enough and open enough to respond to, to affirm and honor the other *as* other. In this way, one "gives life" to the other in her, or his, or its being.

As an analogy to help us understand "releasement," Eckhart would have our heart and mind become as clear and receptive as a mirror whose very being consists in giving the one who gazes into it back to her- or himself. If the mirror is clean and intact, it generally is not noticed by the person gazing into it. She or he tends to be absorbed only in her or his own countenance. A mirror image, Eckhart claims, is essentially not for the mirror but *for* the "other." It directs itself toward the "other" from whom it derives its being. Eckhart suggests that as virgin souls we are called to be like the mirror, to become the conscious space that is empty of self and therefore is free enough to acknowledge and praise God in all of creation. Our freedom from our own agenda, our emptiness as virgin souls, allows us to mirror forth God in all of creation.

In that way, Eckhart continues, all of us are meant to be mothers as well. In released emptiness the virgin receives the mystery revealed in all of creation (including in herself) and in loving gratitude for this—God's gift, the mother bears God back to God.

> Gratitude is the movement from the one who receives to the one who gives. It echoes the goodness of the giver [so that] the giver shines forth from the one who receives. . . . The act of giving into the grateful soul, thus, allows fruit to be born. God gives . . . and receives [God's self] back in the virgin soul who becomes *mother* in *thanks-giving*.[11]

The mystic frequently speaks truth in a deeply symbolic paradox that arises from her or his own experience. For us, thoughts such as these often need time to be absorbed and integrated into our lives. I like to use the symbol of "marinating" for this endeavor. Truly to enter into the meaning of virgin mothering requires inner stillness, *surrendered inwardness*. Eckhart believes that in this inwardness,

> We receive God and become [God's] image. We become, through gratitude, the living reflection, echo, of God. It is here that our fulfillment lies. It is in this, our virginal motherhood, that we are truly free, because, in our total openness, we see the being of all beings flow continuously from the divine abyss. Creation is "nothing" of itself—its being is constant flow outward from God, whose nature is *giving*. This flow outward receives its affirmation in our virgin mothering, because, as human, we can articulate it, and as virgin, we are released toward it.[12]

The movement of releasement intertwined with gratitude liberates us from all divisions and preconceptions of *what should be*, and opens us up to wonder in the face of *what is*. "Things no longer posses us. We stand 'near them but not in them.' We are care-full with things as everything is the gathering place of God."[13]

Eckhart's thoughts awaken us to an extraordinary sense of involvement with the Divine. They are clearly not intended for intellectual speculation and discourse or even argument. Even as I write this, I feel the need for silence and solitude; for space to allow room for the love and gratitude that his insights evoke in me. The rush and noise of everyday life with its worries and concerns seem a clear countermovement to the immersion into depth that our spirit needs and longs for in order to be what we are all called to be. Perhaps Dietrich Bonhoeffer's words can one more time help us to focus on our destiny: "In the birth of Jesus," he tells us, "God took on humanity, not just a single man."[14] The divine breakthrough in all of creation is perhaps more difficult to recognize and accept than God's presence in a single extraordinary person, but clearly we are meant to be part of it.

Releasement and gratitude are for most of us a lifelong challenge. They present a paradox and countermovement especially in our age when the "will to power" is expressed and thoughtlessly justified in so many ways—politics, economics, violence, and especially in war. It is important, therefore, to emphasize that releasement as "letting be" does not imply indifference to evil and cruelty for the sake of control over others. It is not a *laissez-faire* attitude. It shows respect for the person but does not condone the evil she or he is doing or has done. In our age this distinction can easily be overlooked at the expense of human dignity and well-being. Releasement, then, needs to be understood as a strong, unfailing, but also gentle affirmation of the dignity of creation and all creatures. The virgin mother, who all of us (male and female) are called to be, mirrors the Divine and

proclaims the greatness of God. She stands for and works for
justice, pointing unflinchingly in her very being, as did Mary,
the mother of Jesus, to the "collapsing thrones and humbled
lords of this world . . . [to] the power of God and the powerlessness of humankind." She dedicates herself to the task
of transformation, remembering at all times that her model,
Jesus Christ, divine love became "human for all women and
men . . . is not a preacher of abstract ethical ideologies, but
the concrete executor of the love of God."[15]

Thoughts and Questions for Meditation

1. Dietrich Bonhoeffer's meditation on Mary seems to be in
   stark contrast to the rare mention of her in scripture and
   early Christianity. How do you react to this? Does the
   concern with Mary's virginity puzzle you, interest you,
   disturb you? Is this topic relevant to Mary as contemporary Christians might want to understand her?
2. What is your reaction to the reflection concerning marriage and "consecrated" virginity made in the section
   Questions for Our Time?
3. Do you agree with the reflection on "the full and uncompromised humanity of Mary"? How do you relate to
   • the Mother of Jesus beneath the cross,
   • to Mary as the first to "give" Jesus his Body and Blood,
   • to the mystical dimension of Virgin Motherhood—to
     the importance of releasement and gratitude in your
     life?

4

The Experience of Presence

She who gathers together
the many contradictions of her life,
and gratefully embraces them
as one sacred tale,
it is she
who clears the noise-makers from the palace
and celebrates a different feast
where You are the only guest
whom she receives in the softness of evening.
You are the one who shares her loneliness,
the silent center of her monologues.
And each embrace encircling You
stretches her beyond her limitations
into eternity.

Rainer Maria Rilke[1]

Crossing the Divide

The passionate search for truth as a life quest and "release-ment" toward the need to endure the darkness and loneliness of waiting seem rare at best in Western civilization. Among most organized establishments concerned with the deeper questions of life, the Catholic Church, as well as the scientific academy as such (even if not an ever-growing number of scientists as well as Catholic faithful), appear to be two major examples supporting this rarity. Historically they have often been at loggerheads with each other about their diverse convictions, since the need for certitude, order, and finality seems endemic to both. Once something has been accepted by the scientific academy or declared as revealed truth by the established church, it is often deemed inviolable and therefore beyond discussion. Past persecutions of scientists such as Galileo, Giordano Bruno, and others living during the time when temporal power gave the church the ability to silence and oppress them have left serious scars. Science eventually distanced itself from religion, especially during the Enlightenment and the later years of secularization. As a consequence, a certain calcification in worldview and in much that is connected with nature has afflicted religion and its interpretation of reality, so that the distance between both institutions seems, in many respects, to prevail to this day.

It has been suggested that for some scientists of the academy the eagerness in looking for the factual origin of our existence might at least partially or even unconsciously be motivated by the desire to disprove the existence of a "nonmaterial" source rather than simply be an earnest willingness to be open and to embrace whatever will emerge in the research. Could the media frenzy of a few years back around the discovery of the Higgs Boson, dubbed the "God" Boson by some, perhaps be an example of this desire to disprove? An opposite perspective, however, was recently shared with me by a scientist friend. She suggested that probing beyond a certain point in scientific research is something that is only reluctantly addressed, because one might actually encounter what one does not want to address.

Fortunately, I can think of some major exceptions. These, in my estimation, are the *great* scientists, the geniuses especially of the last hundred or so years who have, in fact, crossed the divide. Among them clearly was Albert Einstein, who tirelessly wanted "to know what the 'Old One' thinks," even though his reluctance to "offend" had him deny for a number of years his own discovery of an omnicentric universe—expanding from every point and in all directions. Einstein knew and feared that this discovery (of what the "Old One" thinks) would challenge and endanger the Newtonian "dogma" of established science. Some years later, however, Lincoln Barnett, well known for his study *The Universe and Dr. Einstein,* states quite candidly and fearlessly that "in exploring the macrocosm," one finally comes to "an ultimate, undiversified, and eternal ground beyond which there appears to be nowhere to progress." One "finds barriers on every side and can perhaps but marvel, as St. Paul did nineteen hundred years ago, that 'the world was created by the word of God so that what is seen was made out of things that do not appear.'" Sir James Jeans (astronomer, mathematician, and physicist) claimed he would welcome the spirit "as the creator and ruler of the material realm." Theoretical physicist Walter Heitler postulated an "autonomous and regulating 'spiritual principle' existing outside us." Swiss biologist Adolph Portmann spoke of "an invisible 'abyss of mystery,' containing the structural elements of life, of an 'immense, unknown realm of the mysterious.'"[2] I am sure there are many more, Werner Heisenberg, Max Planck, Wolfgang Pauli, and, of course, Bruce Lipton, among them. Lipton's delightful and groundbreaking study into cell consciousness is, in the words of Karl H. Pribram (neuroscientist), "a much-needed antidote to the 'bottom-up' materialism of today's society."[3]

Sadly, however, even with these developments among scientists, some ecclesial opposition to a rapprochement with science and its discoveries and theories is, nevertheless, still present today. The concern about "conscious evolution" for fear of gnosticism, mentioned in chapter 1, is a case in point. I am at a loss to understand how Cardinal Gerhard Müller, who voiced this concern, can in fact make this connection. I do suspect, however, perhaps incorrectly, that since his statements were made in the context of admonishing the Leadership Conference of Women Religious in the United States who have had a number of speakers addressing this concept, his apprehension may have been caused (consciously or not) by the worry that the sisters might actually start to think beyond "established" norms.[4]

With respect to their interest in "conscious evolution" the women are, of course, in excellent company. Their fascination has been shared, particularly, by Passionist priest Thomas Berry (eco-theologian, cosmologist, earth-scholar) and by Pierre Teilhard de Chardin, S.J. (paleontologist, geologist, and clearly a mystic as well). Both are giants in the field of science and its relation to faith. My own question to Cardinal Gerhard Müller quite humbly would be: to what else can evolution possibly lead if not to ever-wider and deeper consciousness? As Teilhard de Chardin sees it, the evolution of the universe toward ever-greater complexity and consciousness is *empowered* by the drawing force of the Omega Point, who for Teilhard is the Cosmic Christ—supremely conscious and an expression of divine love. This love energy in the universe unites simpler elements, empowering them to "give themselves up in mutual love," as it were, toward ever-greater complexity and beauty: Atom merging with atom into molecules that, in turn, are drawn to unite again toward cells and on to organisms that move toward greater and more profound complexity, opening up to ever-more-conscious life forms. Onward, through the relational power of cosmic love, human beings emerge into self-aware consciousness and are invited to embrace one another in communities empowered by Christ's self-giving love toward deeper and deeper Christification.

Humans, as members in this movement of love, *cannot* and *should not* be understood as separate or as superior. We clearly belong to its dynamic evolution toward the Cosmic Christ, a movement for which we—*conscious, self-aware,* and *free,* are profoundly responsible. This evolutionary process, a holy process, is perhaps best understood as a "from-the-inside-beyond" movement,[5] rather than in terms of a "from-the-outside-in," or a "from-above-to-below" interpretation that has defined our understanding of creation for so long and is ever in danger of envisioning God as the divine craftsman. We in turn, in "His" image, would then see ourselves as in control "over" all other creatures and as working "on" creation as we see fit. We know today what this "from-the-top-down" approach and its inevitable "will to power" has spawned. It is divisive and destructive. Teilhard de Chardin calls it "the ridiculous pretentiousness of human claims to order the life of the world, to impose on the world the dogmas, the standards, the conventions of [humans]."[6] Creation is an ongoing evolving process of which we are an intimate part and in which we thrive. As Teilhard would see it, our acceptance of our responsibility within the evolution of creation toward Christification is akin to discovering fire once again. But this time it is the fire of love, deeply connected to our free "yes."

> Purity does not lie in separation from. . . . It is to be found in the love of that unique boundless essence which penetrates the inmost depths of all things and there, from within those depths, deeper than the mortal zone where individuals and multitudes struggle, works upon them and molds them. Purity lies in a chaste contact with that which is "the same in all."[7]

The Sacred Embrace

My own fascination with the interrelationship of science and spirituality began in the mid-1980s with my reading of Fritjof Capra's *The Tao of Physics*. It was the first book to give me hope that the divide between science and religion regarding the major questions of existence could actually be bridged. As I keep repeating, however, there is this "calcification" that often has organized religion stubbornly claim to *have* the answers formulated centuries and even millennia ago. It holds on to its belief "system" with certainty and often in a language that, in today's different and more developed times, can challenge credibility. Depending on which organized religion one belongs to, this can seriously threaten the membership of those who question and want to probe more deeply and contextually into what has been declared as final and beyond argument. Spiritual writers, therefore, attempting to relate meaningfully to some of today's scientific discoveries, generally avoid the language of strict, specifically dogmatic, theology even if they are familiar with it. My intention and certainly my hope for this reflection on "The Experience of Presence" is to engage the wisdom of science as well as of mystical theology in order to help strengthen the "crossing" over the divide whenever possible and to help us see and experience our fundamental unity.

Fritjof Capra begins his exploration into the *Tao* and its relation to physics by sharing an experience of deep spiritual insight that united "years of study in the area of quantum physics with the deepest of mystical traditions."[8] It happened to him while he, deeply aware of the rhythm of his own breathing, was sitting quietly by the ocean late one afternoon watching the waves roll in.

> I suddenly became aware of my whole environment as being engaged in a gigantic cosmic dance. Being a physicist, I knew that the sand, rocks, water, and air around me were made of vibrating molecules and atoms, and that these consisted of particles which interacted with one another. . . . I knew also that the earth's atmosphere was continually bombarded by showers of "cosmic rays," particles of high energy undergoing multiple collisions as they penetrated the air. All this was familiar to me from my research in high-energy physics, but

until that moment I had only experienced it through graphs, diagrams, and mathematical theories. As I sat on that beach my former experience came to life; I "saw" cascades of energy coming down from outer space, in which particles were created and destroyed in rhythmic pulses; I "saw" the atoms of the elements and those of my body participating in this cosmic dance of energy; I felt its rhythm and I "heard" its sound, and at that moment I *knew* that this was the Dance of Shiva, the Lord of Dancers worshiped by the Hindus.[9]

There is, in my estimation, no true spirituality of Presence that is not directly related to the mystical tradition, be it Christian, Jewish, Sufi, Hindu, Zen, or any other. And what is fascinating about writing on this topic at this time in history is the realization that today, though to some extent still separately, science and mysticism are coming to very similar insights concerning the reality of the universe and our place in it. The unfortunate, hopefully ever-diminishing difference that persists between them is that not everyone can make the connection with the Divine that Capra was "graced" to recognize. Some are simply not free enough to *see* and interpret their discoveries as signposts of the Divine. Out of fear or perhaps because of their "dualistic" training they may resist what others are prepared for and are open to receive. Perhaps Ken Wilber, using the insights of William James, can help clarify the "why" of this: He suggests that James

repeatedly stressed that "our normal waking consciousness is but one special type of consciousness, while all about it parted from it by the filmiest of screens there lie potential forms of consciousness entirely different." It is as if our everyday awareness were but an insignificant island, surrounded by a vast ocean of unsuspected and uncharted consciousness, whose waves beat continuously upon the barrier reefs of our normal awareness, until quite spontaneously, they may break through, flooding our island awareness with knowledge of a vast, largely unexplored, but intensely real domain of new-world consciousness.[10]

What Wilber refers to as "new-world consciousness" is, of course, as old as the mystical tradition throughout the ages of human awareness. Today, however, it slowly seems to be expanding beyond religion proper and ever less frequently needs to fear rejection. It actually seems to grace human consciousness in a multitude of ways. "The most fascinating aspect of such awareness and illuminating experiences," says Wilber, "is that the individual comes to feel, beyond any shadow of a doubt, that he [or she] is fundamentally one with the entire universe, with all worlds, high or low, sacred or profane. [One's] *sense of identity* expands far beyond the narrow confines of [one's] body and embraces the entire cosmos."[11] Mystical, or new-world, consciousness spontaneously and unexpectedly moves us beyond the long-time dualistic boundaries of our Western Greco-Roman worldview and reveals *all* as *one*.

Boundaries isolate us. They have us labor under the illusion of (what the philosopher Kant called) "the categories of our mind," that identify and separate *in* from *out*, *up* from *down*, *forward* from *backward*, *here* from *there*, *far* from *near*, as well as *early* from *late*, *now* from *then*, *present* from *past* and from *future*—all aspects of space and time. Boundaries also provide social divisions that offer such distinctions as *mine* and *yours*, *belonging* and *not belonging*, *superior* and *inferior*, *upper class* and *lower class*, *leader* and *follower*, and so many more. Since ordinary awareness categorizes our experience in this way so that we can function in our "perceived" world, we begin to believe that the boundaries it creates are in fact real; that one side of the division exists autonomously, that is, separate from the other. What a dualistic perspective does not allow us to see, however, is that what we have separated can in fact not exist independently. We cannot have one *without* the other. *In* does not exist alone, nor does *out*. *Up* has no meaning without *down*. *Concave* does not make sense without *convex*.[12] The suffering of *not belonging* makes sense only within the context of *belonging*.

As Wilber sees it, the question "Who am I?," which seems to haunt all of us throughout much of our lives, really has its origin in our propensity to draw boundaries. We want to see ourselves as different from, as unique, as separate—independent from the "you," or "she," or "he," or "they," or "it." But, once again, the "I" does not make sense without the "you," or Martin Buber's "Thou." In my past graduate course on Christian anthropology (nicknamed by my students "Fiand's 'Who am I?' class") I would often start out by dealing with that very question. It is interesting that one can quite easily identify the external aspects or characteristics of oneself: name, function, domicile, nationality, age, gender, education, social and religious affiliations, or connections of one kind or another. If the probing continues, however, one can get rather frustrated because, ultimately, the *who* that I am defies these categories and invites all of us into the mystery of no-*thing*ness, of the intangible, of the "hole in a flute" that Hafiz speaks about, the hole that longs for the breath of the divine flutist who alone is responsible for the music.

This realization can, of course, be ignored or even fought against for quite some time if, in fact, we even allow ourselves to become aware of it. We are not always ready to take the leap into the "absurd," as Kierkegaard understands the "apparent" void that faces us in this experience. Our personal identifications are often quite dear to us, and it may take a heap of suffering before we can realize that they are not what makes us *who we are*; that there is more to us than what they offer. It can be quite disconcerting to let go and freely to move toward the More that seems so illusive, and is literally beyond our ability to identify. For the person of faith, however, its silence and seeming "hiddenness" are really an invitation to open ourselves up to the recognition that, in the final analysis, we do not have within ourselves the reason for our own existence; that there is "Someone" greater who is beckoning us *beyond* the "thingness" of life that seems so important to us and often imprisons us.

Kierkegaard suggested many years ago that the only way to touch that "Someone" is to take the leap into what from a rational point of view does appear to be absurd, but is really the mysterious Source from whom everything that is originates—springs forth—and in whom, in fact, all is held. And so, all the efforts we spend on *filling ourselves up* with titles, and functions, and achievements, and identification marks are wasted if we "hang" the reason for our existence on them, if we depend on them to give us our purpose in life. In the final analysis, as Eckhart invited us to see already in the previous chapter, we are *emptiness waiting to be filled* by the One beyond understanding and categorization, even if we do not necessarily want to admit that. As Francis Thompson would say, We *flee* "Him"—the Source, the Ground of our being,

> down the nights and down the days;
> . . . down the arches of the years;
> . . . down the labyrinthine ways
> of [our] own mind[13]

until finally nothing is left except the divine embrace. In *Embraced by Compassion* I said it this way: "Only when there is nothing left for us to speculate about, and the encounter with the depth of our humanity has rendered us utterly speechless, is there appropriate room for the all-encompassing embrace of the Holy One. Only then, be it in ecstasy or in agony, are we opened to the radical experience of our selves as pointers into the Mystery, no more and no less."[14]

The human journey is strangely paradoxical, and so it happens that when, in fact, we permit ourselves to be still and to listen to the silence, the hunger, and the yearning within, we finally become aware that our finitude and limitedness can, in the last analysis, be recognized and known, can be encountered *only* because the infinite One is already there, waiting for us and beckoning us beyond our limitations. It seems that we hold within ourselves the transcendent—both as the source of our frustrations with our poverty and finitude and also as the ever-empowering hope, as our ultimate destiny. "We are pilgrims," as I mentioned at the beginning of these reflections, "and our home is the heart of God."[15]

Our "graced" loneliness is perhaps best articulated by Karl Rahner, who puts theological categories around Francis Thompson's "The Hound of Heaven." He claims that from the beginning of our individual existence God implants in each of us a hunger that only God can fill.

> Everything else exists so that this one thing might be: the eternal miracle of infinite Love. And so God makes a creature whom God can love: [God] creates [the human being]. [God] creates us in such a way that [we] *can* receive this love which is God himself [herself], and that [we] can and must at the same time accept it for what it is: the very astounding wonder, the unexpected, unexacted gift.[16]

In us, as creation comes to consciousness, its destiny as the expression of divine love calls for a response. We remain lost and lonely, searching for completion, until we recognize our fulfillment in this love affair with the Holy One. It is a gift unconditionally given, a love present from all eternity. Contrary to past theories of salvation, God's love was never lost and does not need to be "bought" back. "We never lose God, so to speak. It is probably much more accurate to say that God 'lost us' and in Christ Jesus came to reclaim us, to remind us of our heritage."[17] God wants to gather us back from our obsession with non-essential self-identifications into an awareness and acceptance of this love. God wants to show us how to abide there, how to make our home there, and how to proclaim with our lives "that this love affair is cosmic, embracing all of creation."[18]

In this respect, Ken Wilber assures us that the "Who am I" question, if pursued beyond the artificial boundaries that we erect for our securities, ultimately will shift us toward a "re-mapping" of our soul that has us "find in it territories [we] never thought possible, attainable, or even desirable." He maintains that

> The most radical re-mapping or shifting of the boundary line occurs in experiences of the supreme identity, for here the person expands his [her] self-identity boundary to include the entire universe. We might even say that [one] loses the boundary line altogether, for when [one] is identified with the "one harmonious whole" there is no longer any outside or inside, and so nowhere to draw the line.[19]

The Benedictine monk and spiritual director Willigis Jäger, when discussing the most important area of agreement between Platonic thought and mysticism, suggests that it is "in the realization that there is no dividing gap between God and the world, that the world is no less than the revelation of the divine and accordingly, that salvation can be understood not as a bridging of a gap but as an awakening to our actual essence."[20] He sees the significance of Jesus as our savior in that he showed us "a way to an experience of unity with the original divine principle."[21] I believe that this experience, as well as our response to, and dwelling in it, is truly our home-coming to the depth of our existence. It is the consolation in what can so often feel like desolation and isolation. In the truest sense, it *is* our salvation; our deepest encounter with a Presence that transcends the boundaries of space and time. Ralph Harper sees it as "a unitary experience and an experience of totality in the midst of [what appear to be] shattering differences. It is the only experience that we can dream of and aspire to that might make it possible for us to live untouched at the core by violence and separation, without losing our minds and our souls."[22] As I wrote elsewhere, this experience of Presence "calls us from within even as it encounters us from without. We touch it at our center and from there are moved beyond ourselves. Unsolicited [and often] unexpected it embraces and holds us, and yet it sets us free. It grounds us and releases us simultaneously."[23]

Beyond Boundaries into the Abyss of Mystery

Re-mapping our soul through a movement beyond illusory boundaries opens our self-identity to an experience of cosmic unity. Boundaries dissolve as it were into one harmonious whole. Ken Wilber calls this an experience of "supreme identity."[24] Within the context of spirituality, an experience such as this opens a place where the world of "reality" and the truth of depth experience merge and explanations yield to silence. The "Who am I?" question, then, probed to its foundation, points to our destiny, to the truth of who we are as surrender. It has us encounter our own "no-*thing*-ness" and acknowledge it as indeed our deepest self—pointing into the divine Mystery that suffuses all of creation as one.

Silence and awe in the face of this unitary experience are clearly the only possible responses. In this regard, as Meister Eckhart maintains, "the highest and loftiest thing that one can let go of is to let go of God for the sake of God."[25] This may seem radical to some; and his prayer, "I pray God to rid me of God,"[26] can be disturbing, unless one realizes that he is referring to our propensity to visualize and define God on our limited and therefore distorted terms, and to absolutize those terms. He prays for the humility to see that anything any of us can ever say about God is at all times limited to our time in history and our very finite understanding. It is tentative at best and should never remain static but should yield to the evolution of consciousness that also always remains finite according to the context of the time in which evolution happens.

Reflection

All of us are called to be faithful to what we have come to understand as our reality in *our* moment in history even as it is unfolding. This is necessary so that we can in fact communicate meaningfully with one another. As I mentioned already, however, this clearly does not always happen in our official church, whose language in many respects continues to hold on to the symbols, and sometimes even the vocabulary, of antiquity. But Latin is not necessarily holier than English, German, Italian, French, or, for that matter, any other contemporary language. The past also is not more sacred than the present, and our attachment to it can at times seriously hinder our experience of the holy in the now. What we proclaim we believe in our creeds (both Nicene and Apostles') on Sunday mornings, for example, is a case in point. Often I find myself mystified as I look around and feel myself surrounded by blank expressions of "disconnect." It seems incongruous to me that at this time in history we still profess to "believe" in

- a fourth-century deity, sitting on a heavenly throne
- at whose right hand sits "his" Son
- who came down to earth to expiate for the sin of our first parent, Adam—tempted by Eve.
- This sin barred all of us from heaven and created a condition of depravity in all of creation
- until restitution was made by God's Son, who alone was capable of doing this (a belief using, at best, a medieval, feudal concept of restitution).
- After this, the Son, having gone "down" to hell (a definite place) to rescue souls waiting for him, ascended

(went "up") to "heaven" (also a definite place) to take his seat next to God.

- We believe that God's Son was born of a virgin who conceived by the power of God's Spirit, with no need of an earthly father.
- We believe in the resurrection of our bodies on the last day,
- when we will all be judged and go to heaven or hell (not a place of waiting, as the one already mentioned, but one of punishment).

Clearly the God of our creeds is a God for ancient times. "He" is far removed from us—above us, a patriarch, a master, a Lord, a creator/maker/craftsman. "He" fits into an ancient monarchical, hierarchical model of society, but not into today and not, for that matter, into mystical thought or depth experience. Even the excuse that when we profess our faith we are obviously speaking symbolically does not help here. Religious symbols are intended to help approximate the sacred for us in our present reality, to enable us to move into sacred space, and, in that way, to open up a unitary experience that brings together the experiential/literal and the mystery that is beyond ordinary understanding. They are meant to make accessible what "in its own reality" defies expression. But when symbols are foreign to our experience, the mystery cannot light up and entice. This clearly is the case with most of our creedal statements. They point to a bygone world that we can only approximate through fantasies or historical novels and movies. Furthermore, the frequent dogmatic insistence on the factual nature of the symbols used destroys their credibility and meaningfulness for today's believer even more. In most respects, then, we need a re-imaging of the Divine—away from the ancient spatial categories of the cosmos, among other things, especially of our earth (flat, with *up* and *down, in* and *out* categories). We know today that the ancient cosmology is no longer valid. The royal pageantry for

God also is foreign to most of us and alienates us from the Divine rather than drawing us toward it.

Immersed in God

But if we return once again to the insights of Teilhard, and if we reflect further on the discoveries of science today, we will find ourselves encountering a God pervading all of creation. For Teilhard, says Ursula King, "the heart at the center of the world is the heart of God."[27] Our heart, as we know, is the primary organ in our bodies. It sends blood throughout our body and gives us life. Because of this, God's heart at the center of the universe can be a depth symbol for us today. It reveals "the most intimate presence whose insertion into the world through the incarnation [means] that the divine runs through all matter and life."[28] Furthermore, this presence of God personalized in Jesus manifests for us, *primarily through the resurrection experience*, a cosmic reality, the Cosmic Christ—divine love embracing all of us and giving us life in a continuous transformative and evolutionary movement.

I saw, as though in an ecstasy, that *through all nature I was immersed in God. . . .* Every element of which I am made up is an overflow from God. When I surrender my self to the embrace of the visible and tangible universe, I am able to be in communion with the invisible that purifies, and to incorporate myself in the Spirit without blemish. . . . God is at work within life. . . . I can feel God, touch [God], "live" [God] in the deep biological current that runs through my soul and carries it with it. . . . God shines through and is personified in humankind. It is God to whom I lend a hand in the person of my fellow [human being]. . . . The deeper I descend into myself, the more I find God at the heart of my being; the more I multiply the links that attach me to things, the more closely does [God] hold me. . . .

"In this first basic vision," comments Ursula King, "we begin
to see how the [reign] of God and the cosmic love may be
reconciled: the bosom of Mother earth is in some way the
bosom of God."[29]

Matter, for Teilhard, is suffused with Spirit. There is here
no room for a dualistic divide. Matter is sacred. It is the
expression of God's love, the evolutionary event of divine cre-
ativity. Matter is the home where God in Christ will express
fulfillment. As Teilhard puts it, "Since immanent progress
is the natural soul of the cosmos, and since the cosmos is
centered on Christ, it must be accepted as proved that, in
one way or another, collaboration with the development of
the cosmos holds an essential and prime position among the
duties of a Christian. It is one single movement that nature
grows in beauty and the body of Christ reaches its full development."[30]

It may be important to clarify here that Teilhard's use
and understanding of the term "Christ" (which many of us
are accustomed to use almost as a surname for Jesus), and
also his use and understanding of "Cosmic Christ," clearly
encompass more than the historical Jesus of Nazareth as
such, even if it is also connected to him as the presencing
of no less than the Divine in human form. What many of
us may not be aware of is that the recognition of Jesus *as*
the Christ by his followers was an event of enlightenment
that occurred some time after his death, very likely over a
period of years and beyond. Today "Christ" has come to be
understood as an integral part of the resurrection experience, which we will reflect on more in detail in a later chapter. Suffice it to say here that the *energy* unleashed in events
after the death of Jesus was enough to bring forth a totally
new way of responding to life, a miracle of transformation, a
moral vision that echoes through the ages and continues to
challenge, as well as inspire, all people of good will even to
this day. Christ, for Teilhard, is the *universal expression and
power of divine love* that encompasses each of us as well as all

of creation. Christ calls us to the task of love, which is meant to bring about unity in fragmentation and division and is moving us toward final Christification, or to what Teilhard calls the Omega Point. Willigis Jäger echoes Teilhard when he claims that for Christians "the term *cosmic Christ* . . . is how we name [the] reality of God that expresses itself in the whole cosmos."[31]

I cannot think of anyone who has been involved with more passion and dedication to the task of "bridging" the divide between spirit and matter arbitrarily established through the centuries than Teilhard de Chardin. Christianity has been buried in the chasm of this divide for centuries. In this way, perhaps unintentionally, it brought about an "undoing" of mystery by "explaining" God, and keeping the distance safely ensconced in intellectual categories and definitions. I suspect that Teilhard's mysticism and the experiential access it offered him to understanding the oneness of spirit and matter also gave him the courage to write what no Catholic unfamiliar with the sciences or with theology *could* have written or (if she or he would have had the familiarity) *would have dared* to write in the time before the Second Vatican Council.

The Seamless Coat of the Universe

What gives validity to Teilhard's mystical vision of unity and the interconnection of everything in the cosmos even to this day is the fact that, from the scientific perspective that has been evolving for the last hundred years or so, separation between anything whatsoever, both with respect to the macrocosm as well as the quantum world, has also ceased to have meaning. As Ken Wilber puts it, "It's not that there are no boundaries between opposites. In a much wider sense, *there are no dividing boundaries between any things or events anywhere in the cosmos.* And nowhere is the reality of no-boundary seen more clearly than in modern physics."[32]

With the dawn of quantum physics in the first quarter of the twentieth century the universally held scientific assumptions of the measurability of all of reality, separated in space and time by various definite boundaries, collapsed. The quantum world offered nothing that the old, treasured Newtonian laws could hold on to. Subatomic particles could not be measured. They could not even be objectively located in space and time. The atom, for example, had for a long time been explained metaphorically as a miniature solar system with some of its components forming the nucleus and others, the "planets," circulating around it. Now, it no longer appeared in any way as a discreet and discernible thing but, as Wilber explains, it "began to look more like a nebulous cloud that infinitely shaded into its environment." Wilber quotes the American physicist Henry Stapp: "An elementary particle is not an independent existing analyzable entity. It is, in essence, a set of relationships that reach outward to other things." And Wilber continues, "These 'atomic things,' the ultimate building blocks of all reality, couldn't be located because, in short, they had no boundaries."[33] Having no boundaries, they also could not be measured or numbered; nor could any clear laws be established for them. The best quantum physics can work with now is probabilities and statistics. What the quantum perspective reveals to us is that

> What were once thought to be bounded "things" turned out to be interwoven aspects of each other. For some strange reason, every thing and event in the universe seemed to be interconnected with every other thing and event in the universe. The world, the real territory, began to look not like a collection of billiard balls but more like a single, giant, universal field, which Whitehead called the "seamless coat of the universe." ... Physicists], it seems, succeeded in catching a glimpse of the real world, the territory of no boundary,

. . . the world as it is and not as it is classified, bounded, mapped, meta-mapped.[34]

Though Wilber in these observations does not speak specifically to the unity of spirit and matter, his discussion on cosmic interconnectivity and the apparent "boundary-lessness" in the subatomic world at least seems to narrow the gap, and to acknowledge the mystery that opens up when research approaches, what he calls, "the real world, the territory of no boundaries." There is in what Wilber writes here also an affinity with Teilhard's thought: Wilber mentions that Teilhard "speaks of this seamless coat" that Whitehead identified, and then quotes Teilhard directly: "Considered in its concrete reality, the stuff of the universe cannot divide itself. . . . The farther and more deeply we penetrate into matter, . . . the more we are confounded by the interdependence of its parts. . . . It is impossible to cut into this network, to isolate a portion without it becoming frayed and unraveled at all its edges."[35]

Perhaps no scientist has more honestly admitted to the ultimate mystical insights that cannot but emerge when we earnestly pursue the question of existence than has Sir Arthur Eddington, an astronomer, physicist, and mathematician of the early twentieth century, who did his greatest work in astrophysics. When commenting on the book *Quantum Questions: Mystical Writings of the World's Great Physicists*, he points out that "each of these remarkable men, without exception, came to believe in a mystical or transcendental worldview that embodies the world as a spiritual, rather than material phenomenon."[36] Ken Wilber, who edited the book, summarizes Eddington's view that physics, as a discipline, is merely a "partial aspect" pointing to "something wider." Wilber explains, "Physics deals with shadows; to go beyond shadows is to go beyond physics; to go beyond physics is to head toward the meta-physical or mystical—and *that* is why so many of our pioneering physicists were mystics. The new physics contributed nothing positive to this mystical venture, except a spectacular failure, from whose smoking ruins the spirit of mysticism gently arose."[37]

Physics today speaks of the boundless, of something wider, immeasurable, and *beyond its ability to grasp.* Spirituality speaks of the infinite—the endless, unlimited, immeasurable. Both point to the mystery that defies understanding. Mystics encounter this mystery in the silence of their prayer and see "as though in an ecstasy, that through all nature [they are] immersed in God." Having to "face" that which their discipline and its methods cannot reach, physicists, on the other hand, politely stand back and accept that this mysterious "more" is "non-visible, non-visualizable even. It defies measurability, time and space, and yet, its existence, though beyond their expertise to know, cannot be denied."[38]

There are, nevertheless, numerous speculations among the scientific "greats" about this "more." Brian Swimme refers to it as the "unseen ocean of potential . . . an infinity of pure generative power."[39] Ervin Laszlo speaks of the "quantum vacuum" and sees it as "the energy and information filled plenum that underlies our universe, and all universes" in what he calls "the Metaverse."[40] Professor of physics John Hagelin, in an interview connected to the movie *What the Bleep!? Down the Rabbit Hole: One Movie; Infinite Possibilities,* calls the mysterious ultimate reality "the unified field of pure consciousness," and understands it as pure potentiality, the fountainhead of all that is. A term often used by many physicists in trying to speak about the non-visualizable or unfathomable is the "field." The purpose of this book discourages a lengthy discussion into the theories around the "field." I have dealt with it somewhat in two previous publications and refer the interested reader to *Awe-Filled Wonder: The Interface of Science and Spirituality* (Paulist Press) and *From Religion Back to Faith: A Journey of the Heart* (Crossroad Publishing Co.). Suffice it here to say that *the* field underlying all other fields refers to a domain beyond space-time and is the unchanging depth dimension of everything that appears, has appeared, and will appear in the observed world. It is not merely one among others. It is "the ultimately real dimension of the cosmos." It is "the ground for the existence of everything, including ourselves."[41]

Spirituality and mystical thought would very likely understand this "field" as "the mind of God," or perhaps the "heart of God." Ervin Laszlo relates the "field" to the Hindu understanding of the Akasha, which he identifies as "a dimension in the universe that subtends all the things that exist in it." It also "generates and interconnects all things, and it conserves the information they have generated. It is the womb of the world, and the memory of the world."[42] When asked whether what he was referring to was spiritual, Laszlo answered that the new world paradigm emerging at this time overcomes the "specious divide" between spirituality and science. "Genuine spirituality has always been based on the recognition of a deeper intelligence at work in the cosmos." In the same way, "A mature science recognizes that the world is far greater and deeper than our sensory experience of it. . . . A mature science is spiritual, and a mature religion is scientific. They are built on the same experience, and they reach basically the same conclusion."[43]

When we forget our humanity, our finitude, and our limitations, we fail to see that we are meant to be community, to reach beyond the illusion of separateness and search together for the depth that supports us all. Human arrogance is at the root of all division and strife. But we cannot go it alone. We are held in love as the binding force that ultimately eliminates our blindness and faces us with the reality of our fundamental oneness. The recognition among scientists and spiritual writers that their diverse paths lead to the same conclusions, and that the hunger that drives them comes from the same source, is one major step toward eliminating our human alienation and lostness, and bringing us to the same table—one human family, reconciled.

The Evolution of Consciousness

This has been by far the longest chapter so far, and as I am reflecting on the "why" of this, it occurs to me that as we search and struggle for an understanding of our faith in the twenty-first century, it is essential that we reflect deeply on where we are today, both individually and culturally, in our attempt to transcend dualism toward an integrated world perspective.

I devoted a lengthy section in my previous book, *Embraced by Compassion,* to an exploration into the movement of individual human maturation and conscious evolution from

1. coenesthesis and the symbiotic union with one's mother, where the "I" is deeply enmeshed with its maternal source,
2. to a progressive separation occurring during the onset of ego awareness (the beginning of the "who am I?" questions discussed earlier) and its subsequent functional and boundary-conscious approach to the world.
3. This eventually, and through progressive phases of growth, opens up to what Jung referred to as the "second journey," and what Laszlo identifies as "transpersonal consciousness," signaling ultimately the depth call to maturation and wholeness.[44]

Numerous thinkers and writers have addressed this personal journey. Many have also drawn comparisons between individual and cultural maturation. Some theories are highly complicated, while others are more accessible to those simply seeking help in understanding their own experience and struggle.[45] All, however, invariably suggest that human consciousness, whether individual or cultural, is destined to

evolve toward an ever-more-profound experiential understanding of our at-oneness with the universe and with one
another. A number of thinkers also express a view with which
I strongly agree, namely, that no stage in this evolutionary
process is ever left behind completely; rather it is integrated
into the next level and adapted to a wider vision.

It is important to note that especially in the case of the
more advanced levels of maturation (stages 2 and 3 mentioned above) when the previous level of development
reaches its own end point or limit, there usually follows a
period of resistance to further growth and a desire to stay
put. But as scripture tells us (Hebrews 13:14), "we have
not here a lasting city," and so, after what can be a painful
struggle with "existential boredom" and lost-ness that can
at times endanger further growth by having us succumb to
fixation and eventual regression, authentic maturation calls
us to let go, to integrate what has gone before, and gradually
to move toward the next level of consciousness.

Reflection

A Dream

I was in my early forties when I found myself in the midst of
the struggle just described, and so familiar to those who have
journeyed into the second half of life. Resistance and frustration had been intense, as was the subsequent struggle with
meaninglessness, with apparent loss and the wonder about
what life is really all about.

Then one night I had a dream.

I found myself traveling in a crowded streetcar through
the cobblestone streets of my hometown in Germany. My
misery was intense, but here I was—in my beloved Freiburg,
trying desperately to get a hold on my loneliness, and doubt-
ful that I would ever find myself again. It was a hot sum-
mer day, and the streets were busy with shoppers and tour-

ists whom I barely noticed. And then, all of a sudden, *there it was*: the beautifully laced, 700-year-old sandstone spire of the *Münster*,* majestically rising above the buildings, the busy streets and noise outside. Silently and gracefully it pointed heavenward into the mystery of an ever-evolving universe beckoning me and gently touching my inner misery and pain.

I struggled through the crowd of passengers, found my way to the door and open platform, jumped from the moving streetcar and started to run feverishly through the narrow streets. My only goal: to get there, to *be* there, to touch it, to have its sacred presence envelop me, to come *home*, to be *whole*. Breathless and trembling, I finally arrived at the large entrance. I threw my arms around one of its giant pillars and stood there, pressing my forehead against its cool, deep red stone.

And then I woke up, *weeping*.

The meaning of life gifts us as, in agony or in ecstasy, we surrender to its mystery. It embraces us as we allow its holiness to pervade our yearning, our striving, and our longing for the depths of its "living waters." They are there, have been there, and always will be there to quench our thirst, if we but courageously and faithfully seek understanding.

Though the theories on conscious evolution vary on specific details, Ervin Laszlo finds that they do "have a common thrust." They all agree that conscious evolution is from ego-bound, dualistic, boundary-obsessed consciousness to the transpersonal, holistic form. "If this is so," Laszlo con-

----

*"*Münster*" refers to the Gothic cathedral of Freiburg i.Br., in the Black Forest region of southern Germany. Its ancient tower is more than 380 feet high. Its construction was completed in 1330 CE, after 130 years. The *Münster* was one of the few structures that miraculously remained standing after the firebombing of the inner city at the end of the Second World War in 1944. For me it is a symbol of abiding holiness in the midst of chaos and destruction.

tinuous, "it is the source of great hope. . . . It could produce greater empathy among people, and greater sensitivity toward animals, plants, and the entire biosphere. . . . It could change our world."[46]

I must admit that writing about the transformation and evolution of human consciousness midway into the second decade of the twenty-first century can appear somewhat unrealistic. Today we have to face terrorism "in the name of religion" that seriously threatens civilization worldwide. There are enormous tensions and violence afflicting much of the Middle East as well as large sections of the African continent. We witness internal and external violence in the Ukraine. The European Union is struggling to survive in the face of economic disparity and pressures. Prejudice is rearing its ugly head in numerous venues. Our planet's wildlife, air, and oceans are suffering from rampant pollution and climate change caused, in large part, by our refusal to face our excesses. In the light of all this and so much more, the transformation of cultural as well as individual consciousness seems rather tenuous to say the least.

I have to encourage myself, as I reflect on what I have just written, that what is happening today may very likely be the cultural equivalent (for our time) of the individual and deeply personal crisis that precedes deeper integration for each one of us. Cultures, even more so than individuals, also struggle with resistance and inner turmoil before darkness yields to dawn. The claim that "we have always done it this way" is a strong argument and motivation not to change. For many structures and institutions today, including governments, transformation carries with it what can appear like major losses. Materialism, industrialism, consumerism, nationalism, patriarchy, individualism, racism, and the prejudice that can make the advantaged feel so comfortably superior to others, all have a lot to give up for the sake of greater love. When conscious evolution has not yet reached the turning point, or what some call the "critical mass," it can seriously threaten the status quo. It asks for surrender, and sometimes can appear all too costly when "goals that serve all peoples and countries of the world, whatever their creed, level of economic development, population size, and natural resource endowment"[47] start to emerge as priorities, and the rights of all people ask to be respected. It is therefore not uncommon that resistance to change can be quite strong and lead to violent acts.

But good ideas and prophetic visions should not be ignored because they are unpopular and challenge the status quo. The ethical genius is rarely popular and often persecuted and even killed. Jesus is likely the best example for us. His vision was not too different from what Laszlo presents here. And as Christians we might well ask ourselves why, as members of what is still the largest religion in the world, so many of us do not fully endorse *with our lives* the vision of transformation Jesus preached and Laszlo is describing. I often ask those present on retreats I am asked to offer whether they think the world is a better place because of Christianity. It is easy to give a quick and perhaps unreflective affirmative reply to this question. But is it? Perhaps an even more provocative question for each of us could be whether the world is in fact better because I am Christian or, closer to home, whether my community, my neighborhood, my parish, my family is better, happier, kinder or more charitable, because I am a Christian. It would seem that the Buddhist mystic Thich Nhat Hanh might be more aware than many of us of our universal interconnectedness and, therefore, of the personal responsibility each one of us bears for conscious evolution or the lack thereof in all of creation. Faced with the turmoil and violence raging throughout the world, he saw himself connected to it all, and so, when he was asked who caused the war in Iraq, for example, he is reported to have quickly responded, "I did."

Laszlo, in his description of a society imbued with transpersonal consciousness, clearly is presenting a very challenging and different picture from the one we are experiencing today. He describes it as one where "disparities in wealth and power would be moderated and frustration and resentment would diminish, together with crime, terrorism, war, and other forms of violence. Societies would become more peaceful and sustainable, offering a fair chance of life and well-being to all their members, living and yet to be born."[48] He is, however, not naïve, since he follows this description by observing that from today's perspective what he has just described is "distinctly utopian." (*It, of course, is Christian, as well.*) Laszlo also warns,

> Evolution is never fully predictable. All we can say is that if humankind does not destroy its life-supporting environment and decimate its populations, the dominant consciousness of a critical mass will evolve from the ego-bound to the transpersonal stage. This evolution is certain to leave its mark on people and societies.
>
> When our children and grandchildren graduate to transpersonal consciousness, an era of peace, fairness, and sustainability could dawn for humanity.[49]

His remarks should be encouraging when we realize that according to *The World Factbook* the percentage of Christians in the world today, including all denominations, is 31.5 percent. The question, however, needs to be whether our presence in such large numbers has significantly changed human behavior for the better? This is a challenge for all of us as we ask ourselves how the vision of Jesus has in fact been lived.

In a short reflection by Thich Nhat Hanh entitled "Jesus Needs Christians," and found in his book *Living Buddha, Living Christ*, he wrote,

> For the Buddha to be present in the Sangha (community), we must practice in a way that keeps his teachings alive, and not confined to sermons and scriptures. The

best way a Buddhist can keep the teachings of the Buddha alive is to live mindfully in the way the Buddha and his community lived. For Christians, the way to make the Holy Spirit truly present in the church is to practice thoroughly what Jesus lived and taught. It is not only true that Christians need Jesus, but Jesus needs Christians also for His energy to continue in this world.[50]

Thoughts and Questions for Meditation

1. What is your response to the observation in "Crossing the Divide" about the relationship between the Catholic Church and the scientific academy and scientists in general? Do you have any experience (for or against) in this regard?
2. How do you relate to the discussion on conscious evolution?
3. Can you relate to the notion of universal interconnectivity and the responsibility it imposes on us as "creation come to consciousness"?
4. Are you comfortable with the distinctions drawn in this chapter between Jesus of Nazareth, historically understood, and the Cosmic Christ?
5. What is your response to Ken Wilber's explanation of our propensity to establish boundaries and to separate what really cannot exist apart?
6. Does the mysticism of the great scientists mentioned in this chapter surprise you, puzzle you, excite you, give you hope?
7. How does the depth approach to the "Who am I?" question, which moves beyond categories of self-identification, affect you?
8. Do you relate to the discussion of the stages in maturation and conscious evolution in your own personal life?

Where do you see it in our culture? Where do you see its absence and the need for major transformation?

9. Do you relate to the experience of crises in this process of cultural evolution, and do you think the violence in our time may be due to (conscious or unconscious) resistance to, and fear of, the emergence of a deeper and more compassionate humanity?

10. In the light of Laszlo's observation regarding "the dominant consciousness of a critical mass," what is your response to Thich Nhat Hahn's statement that "Jesus needs Christians"?

5

Be What You See, Become What You Are

When I imagine myself as an old woman [man] at the end of my life and ask myself how I will evaluate my time here, there is only one question that concerns me: Did I love well? There are a thousand ways to love other people and the world—with our touch, our words, our silence, our work, our presence. I want to love well. This is my hunger. I want to make love to the world by the way I live in it, by the way I am with myself and others every day. So I seek to increase my ability to be with the truth in each moment, to be with what I know, the sweet and the bitter. I want to stay aware of the vastness of what I do not know. This is what brings me to the journey. I do not want to live any other way.

And sometimes, I allow myself to imagine that each moment in which we love well by simply being all of who we are and being fully present allows us to give back something essential to the Sacred Mystery that sustains all life.[1]

Oriah Mountain Dreamer

Jesus Needs Christians

In his "Letter from Rome" of February 18, 2015, Robert Mickens tells of Msgr. Pietro Sigurani (affectionately referred to as Don Pietro by his parishioners), who, at age seventy-six, was forced to retire from his parish (Nativity of Jesus Christ) where he had served for thirty-seven years, turning it into one of the most dynamic parishes in the diocese. He was subsequently appointed as rector of the Church of Sant'Eustachio, "one of the hundreds of 'museum churches' that decorate Rome's historic center, an area where local residents are too few to be able to support them as vibrant parishes." Mickens reports that since Don Pietro's reassignment in 2012, he has transformed Sant'Eustachio into a vibrant center for prayer and theological-sociological dialogue. What is most exciting to me, however, is that he also has turned this "museum church" into a welcome place for Rome's poor and marginalized. Over a hundred people are brought in daily from Rome's outskirts by Don Pietro's "Friends of Sant'Eustachio." They are seated in the central nave of this magnificent historic place of worship, which serves as their dining room. There they are served a hot and nourishing meal. They tell their Don Pietro: "We eat like the rich and important people here—in a grand palace!" And that was, of course, one of the priest's main objectives—"to bring the poor to the center of our attention, the center of the city of Rome and the center of Italy's palace of power." Don Pietro believes that "the house of God is where the poor should be fed!"[2]

When I first read Mickens's deeply touching story my immediate response was, This is what Jesus wanted. *This* is eucharist—a magnificent expression of what he claimed as "the new covenant in my blood." In his brief but powerful study on *The Future of the Eucharist*, Bernard Cooke points out,

Accepting this covenant enacted in eucharist, a covenant focused on the risen Christ present to the community as the living pledge that unites humans and God, means that those sharing eucharist share also in the pledge. Like the ancient baptismal formula that forbade discrimination in the church between rich or poor, slave or free, Jew or Gentile, male or female, today's eucharist calls Catholics to honor and implement the absolute equality of all persons by working to abolish discriminations. Like the covenant of Israel that fixed just relations among humans as the measure of their relation to God, the eucharistic community itself is meant by its pursuit of justice to be a sacrament of humanity's relationship to God.[3]

Cooke observes that one's pledge to the authentic character of the eucharistic liturgy makes the commitment to social justice unavoidable.

Reflection

In the light of this, one might ask what it would be like if the poor at Sant'Eustachio were interviewed about their marital status prior to the meal and were denied food if they were divorced and remarried. It boggles my mind that the episcopate of our church at this time in history spends days debating exclusion from the eucharistic table and uses Jesus's words against divorce, which were clearly aimed at the misogyny of his time, as justification for its concern. Jesus's teaching about open table fellowship in Luke 14:12-24 illustrates the radical inclusivity Jesus advocated for the reign of God. His emphasis is primarily on the poor, infirm, and outcasts. Ultimately, though, he included anyone found in the lanes and roads without any regard to their "social standing"—something so extremely important in the culture of his day. As

John Dominic Crossan observes, "It is the random and open commensality of the parable's meal that is the most startling element. One could in such a situation have classes, sexes, ranks, and grades all mixed up together. The social challenge of such egalitarian commensality is the radical threat of the parable's vision."[4] The negative reaction was, of course, predictable: Jesus is depicted as "a glutton, a drunkard, and a friend of tax collectors and sinners. He makes, in other words, no appropriate distinctions and discriminations. He has no honor. He has no shame."[5]

What for me is perhaps one of the most remarkable aspects of Jesus's stance vis-à-vis the ritual laws of his culture and his religion is that, according to Crossan, "He did not care enough about [them] either to attack or to acknowledge them. He ignored them, but that, of course, was to subvert them at a most fundamental level. . . . Open commensality profoundly negates distinctions and hierarchies between female and male, poor and rich, Gentile and Jew. It does so, indeed, at a level that would offend the ritual laws of *any* civilized society. That was precisely its challenge."[6]

If, in the light of this reflection, we return once more to Thich Nhat Hahn's observation with which we ended the previous chapter: "For Christians, the way to make the Holy Spirit truly present in the church is to practice thoroughly what Jesus lived and taught"; our challenge is great. Obedience (largely unquestioned) for Catholics has been a highly prized virtue. Serious sin was often associated with ignoring it, and, in many respects, the hierarchical structure of our church has survived because of it.

I know of a pastor who some years ago was ordered by his ordinary to deny communion to those in his parish who were divorced and remarried. He had apparently been reported as not having paid much attention to this rule. On the following Sunday, he decided to warn his parishioners of the order given to *him*, and then he informed them where in the sanctuary among all the other distributers (who had not received this order) *he* would be distributing. I know of another pastor who sent a registered letter to a couple who had married after both had been divorced from a previous marriage. They had until then gone to receive the eucharist during Sunday liturgy as usual. The letter informed them that if they tried to receive communion again, he would openly refuse the sacrament to them. Who of the two pastors, I wonder, made the Holy Spirit truly present in the church? Who helped Christ's energy to be truly active and alive among his people?

I Have Set You an Example

As I already mentioned, many New Testament stories, though not all, were parabolic rather than strictly historical-factual attempts to tell us *who* Jesus was and *what* he was about. The New Testament is not, nor does it need to be, primarily and strictly historical or biographical in order to speak the Christian message and mandate. What then was Jesus primarily about? What, once again, strikes me most forcefully as I meditate on the Gospel stories is the almost universal message of unconditional forgiveness, as well as total inclusivity and acceptance on the part of Jesus. From the Christmas parables onward, throughout his life, to his last meal with his disciples, and even during the agony on the cross as well as in the accounts after his resurrection, forgiveness, acceptance and inclusion of outcasts, women, and foreigners seem to predominate. The following stories are particularly dear to me in the way they illustrate the Christian mandate Jesus calls us to imitate.

A Meditation

- *Zacchaeus, the tax collector*

The first is the account of Zacchaeus, a tax collector—a profession infamous for exploitation and despised by all. He

it is with whom Jesus decides to have dinner. As the story has
it, the man simply wants to satisfy his curiosity and to have a
look at the famous healer. He climbs a tree for a better view
because he is small in stature and, I suppose, also to avoid
the unfriendly crowd. When Jesus looks up, sees him, and
invites himself and his friends to dinner at his house, the man
is overjoyed, hurries home, and prepares a sumptuous feast.

And here my imagination takes over: Zacchaeus, shunned
and hated by everyone for his heartlessness and dishonesty,
feels included by these strangers. No one preaches to him
about his sinfulness. No one looks down on him or seems
to despise him. They are all a happy, hungry, and friendly
group, laughing and telling stories. He feels accepted unconditionally as one of them, included in the merry-making.
And in the midst of this acceptance and care and, most likely,
because of it, Zacchaeus experiences conversion. The man literally "goes to confession" and pledges to change his life. We
see here none of the "confession first, followed by obliga-
tory penance, after which the meal is once again available to
the sinner." There is no open judgment or condemnation on
the part of Jesus, who simply and lovingly sees Zacchaeus
as a son of Abraham and Sarah—as his brother, a child of
God. The Christian mandate is unconditional acceptance of
others, not necessarily of what they do, but of *them.* Love
entices and can change hearts. "Love your neighbor as you
love yourself."

- *Breaking bread with Judas*

But even in other stories when conversion is not forth-
coming, Jesus still breaks bread and reaches out. He shares
his last meal with Judas, whom, as the stories would have it,
he knows to be his betrayer.

- *The thief on the cross*

The "thief" on the cross is not asked whether he is truly
sorry for what he has done but is promised total acceptance

and welcome in the next life—that very day. There is no demand for penance, no purgatory waiting for him on the other side.

- *The executioners*

Those who nail Jesus to the cross are not condemned for the horror and pain they inflict. He simply asks God to forgive them.

These are extraordinary stories that leave no room for argument as to what authentic Christianity is all about. I suppose one could claim that when one has a system or an institution to run there need to be rules and regulations; that one can simply not tolerate or ignore the sin. Jesus, of course, did not tolerate or ignore the sin either. He simply *loved* the sinner. But then, he also did not "run an institution," and that can give us pause.

- *Breakfast at the seashore*

Perhaps one more story will stretch and challenge us even further: It is a post-resurrection story that I affectionately call "breakfast at the seashore." The disciples had gone back to Galilee, back to what they had been about before Jesus had entered their lives. Despondent, I am sure, and wondering whether it had all been a dream, they had gone fishing and, after a night of hard work, had caught nothing. And then, there he was, helping them to a great catch, and when they came to shore he had breakfast for them. The tenderness of this scene is so deeply touching! They had slept through his agony and fear, too tired and perhaps confused and fear-filled themselves to give support. And then, when he was arrested, all had deserted him. Their loyalty and friendship were truly questionable, but *never* his love for them.

After breakfast he went on a walk with Peter—two friends needing reassurance. One was terribly ashamed; the other simply needed to renew the old bond. "Peter do you love me?" he asked tenderly. Peter, I imagine, *groaned* his response: "Yes, Lord, you know how very much I love you." One can certainly pause here and dwell in that experience— gently and compassionately recalling the betrayals in one's own life. What follows in the story, however, still demands our attention, especially in the light of the previous reflection on our, and therefore our church's, attitude toward the sinner among us. The story tells us that Jesus, in fact, and without any further condition, asked Peter to be the leader of the group. How could he have done that after all that had happened?

There is, I believe, a profound paradox with respect to sin; how knowing it and acknowledging one's own weakness can liberate us and open us to compassion. I think that Jesus knew that good leadership comes from a deep-down knowledge of one's own brokenness and personal need for mercy and healing. Too exalted a view of one's own excellence seems to me an obstacle to true leadership. Even if, as is often the practice in ecclesial ministry, one attributes one's "higher" state to a divine calling and therefore somehow an unearned gift, a lack of awareness of one's own brokenness can easily have one succumb to intolerance and arrogance. What can be missing is the compassion and understanding of others. No good leader can afford that. Recognizing that one has "been there, done that" helps the leader to walk that extra mile and help carry the load.

Take, Bless, Break, Share

This has been a long meditation on the essential Christian message of inclusion and acceptance. The primary symbol for this, as depicted in the life of Jesus, is the meal. Shared meals in the culture of the day, as Richard McBrien tells us, "signified peace, trust, and community." The "shared meals with sinners, outcasts, and tax collectors" were Jesus's way of demonstrating "that the reign of God had begun, was open to all, and demanded love of all."[7] Jesus, of course, during his public ministry shared many meals, some as a guest, like the one with Zacchaeus and the ones in Bethany. Others were on his own initiative. Aside from the Last Supper with his friends, which we have come to see as the one we celebrate in memory of him at the eucharist, the Gospels focus our attention also on what John Dominic Crossan calls the "bread and fish Eucharists,"[8] two of which are reported in Mark 6 and John 6 as happening before his death and resurrection. These were the meals with large crowds of several thousand people and the disciples having just five loaves and two fish to share. Since it turned out that all present had enough to eat, however, and there was even food left over, we can surmise quite simply that the sharing modeled by Jesus and his disciples encouraged others to do the same. *That*, in itself, could be considered a miracle.

There are a number of bread-and-fish eucharists with Jesus after the resurrection as well. None apparently involved wine. Bread-and-fish eucharists also are depicted "in paintings on the walls of the earliest Christian catacombs in Rome . . . [and in] early Christian funerary carvings and inscriptions."[9] Crossan, along with Richard Hiers and Charles Kennedy, whom Crossan cites in the above research, considers it, therefore, as "fairly certain . . . that either for Jesus himself or for quite early, and probably, Jewish Christians, the meal of bread and fish, of which we learn in the gospels, was understood as a eucharistic anticipation . . . [of] the blessed life of table fellowship in the Kingdom of God."[10]

If this is surprising and somewhat confusing for some, it may be helpful to remember that Jesus and most of his followers were of the peasant and working class of that time. Wine was not part of their regular meals. Important also is our continued focus on the inclusiveness and self-gift of Jesus's life symbolized by the *shared* meal: take, bless, break, and share (regardless of the menu). It is *there* where, after the resurrection, his followers and all of us even now can experience that he is with us still. Losing this focus and replacing the experience with the need for a definition of objective reality blinds us to the depth of his presence and to the importance he placed on the common bond of our humanity. There were, then, two different traditions in the very early Jesus movement. One anticipated the Kingdom of God with a shared meal of bread and fish, the other at the "Last Supper," with the breaking of bread and sharing the cup of wine. The latter eventually, and very likely with the development of a gentile Christian Church, took ascendency, so that today few of us are even aware of the former.

Crossan leaves his reflection on these different traditions with the following observation: "It might be considered, however, whether bread and fish *for the crowd* and abundant fragments left over is a better ritualization of Jesus' own life than bread and wine *for the believers* with abundance now completely irrelevant."[11] In the light of the culture in which Jesus lived, the meal of bread and fish might indeed have been the one dearer to him. It was, after all, inclusive of both "have and have-nots," available to everyone, and clearly open to abundance. Wine, on the other hand, in the peasant culture in which Jesus was at home, was for the festive occasion, for the few or the wealthy; not for all at all times. In fact, for most people it was rare, if ever. The meal Jesus had in mind was to be available for everyone without exception.

Regarding early eucharistic meals, it is important furthermore to remember that "special status" in the Jesus community after the resurrection was not immediate. Final rules concerned with the ritual as well as the reception of and eligibility for the communal meal of remembrance were formulated in the course of history, even though they may often have been proclaimed "in the name of Jesus." I suggest that they actually would have been uncomfortable for, and certainly foreign to, the itinerant preacher from Palestine who "came" so that *all* might "have life and have it in abundance" (John 10:10).

As Bernard Cooke points out:

> Popular understanding has tended to view the Last Supper as "the first Mass" and even see it as the occasion when Jesus ordained his disciples as "the first priests." Neither of these is accurate. Jesus did not himself establish any ritual forms of Christianity, nor did he ordain anyone. Historical research into the origins of Christianity makes it rather clear that ritual forms like the eucharist only gradually came into being in the first few decades of the church.[12]

The sacramental theologian Kenan B. Osborne places the origin of the eucharist as well as baptism in the time of Jesus or, at least, the apostolic period.[13] To repeat, however, the rituals for these celebrations, as well as for the other sacraments, underwent numerous changes through the years. They were clearly not introduced by Jesus. With reference to priesthood, Osborne (drawing on the *Apostolic Tradition* of Hippolytus [c. 215], which gives "the first extant indication of ordination and its ritual") places both ordination and the anointing of the sick around 200 CE.[14] As far as the necessity for ordination in order to preside at the eucharist is concerned, not until the year 1208 by Innocent III "is there an official declaration that priestly ordination is necessary to celebrate the Eucharist."[15] This regulation was later reinforced by the Council of Florence (1430) and also by the Council of Trent (1563).

A simple ritual practice for the celebration of the eucharist was of course already present in the communities of the first century although it was still quite fluid. After the death and resurrection of Jesus, as the communities became larger, the person presiding at the meal very likely would have been the one in whose home the gathering took place. There was then, as Crossan describes it,[16] a slow and diversified formalization of the meal practice of Jesus whose vision for an inclusive, mutually supportive community symbolized by open commensality gradually moved from the bread-and-fish meal of abundance to a more boundary conscious and also more ritualized service of bread and wine with eventual reference to membership through baptism and a possible need for repentance (*Didache* 9:5; 10:6b). There was still, however, no immediate nor universal reference to a Passover meal or passion symbolism (which may not have been universally known). Finally, formalization became more and more universal.

As Tad W. Guzie points out in his thoughtful and informative study on the eucharist:

> There are very good historical indications that the account of the last supper did not become a regular part of christian eucharistic prayers until sometime during the second century. The earliest christians probably "worded" their eucharist with a series of thanksgivings modeled on the Jewish thanksgiving prayers used at ritual meals. . . . Specific reference to the last supper developed later, as christianity separated more and more from judaism and as need developed to state the specifically christian meaning of the eucharistic meal.[17]

Guzie argues convincingly that when Paul, whose references to the eucharist are among the earliest, recounts the actions and recites the words of Jesus at the Last Supper in 1 Corinthians 11:23-26 he is not yet, at that early stage, referring to a "liturgical text, not a text used in the eucharistic action itself." He is rather instructing the Corinthians about what they should already have known, lived, "and kept in mind during worship because it interprets what christians are doing when they gather for their ritual meal."[18] Paul's letter to them was a reminder of his earlier catechesis, which they seemed to have forgotten. It was written out of concern for the Christian community that appeared to have lost the

spirit of shared commensality and compassion so important
to Jesus. Although they would have broken bread and shared
the cup at the end of the meal in remembrance of Jesus, they
ignored each other prior to that and humiliated those who
had nothing to eat during the actual time for eating before
the eucharist. Guzie points out Paul's concern that "they
were forgetting the indissoluble connection between their
meal and the death of Jesus."[19]

Here again, it would seem, that right from the beginning,
and even as the ritual celebration was still in its beginning
and only slowly developing, the emphasis was on *action* and
never merely on concepts, on definitions, or on words that
alone were purported to have power. Eucharist in the early
Christian community emphasized the unity of life in Christ,
witnessed through self-giving love and compassion.

Edward Schillebeeckx, speaking to the Pauline tradition as
primary in the development of our eucharistic understanding, stresses

> that the development of the interpretation of the "cel-
> ebration of a meal with Jesus" in the primitive Church
> was parallel to that of a progressive penetration into the
> mystery of Christ. Originally, the emphasis was not on
> *interpreting* this meal, but on celebrating and experi-
> encing it. In celebrating this meal, early Christians had
> the experience of being a Church—an eschatological
> community on the basis of their personal relationship
> with Jesus, whom they had come to know explicitly as
> Christ in the resurrection.[20]

"The actions done with bread and wine," then, were for
the early followers of Jesus a way "to say that *their* existence
and search for the [reign] of God was bound up with himself."[21] His food—that which gave him life and energy and
perseverance even in the face of utter rejection, was to do the
will of his Abba. He was born for this, united to it. He lived

for it and was ready to give up his life for it. We, as his followers are called to the same.

Sacrifice

Although Christians, at some point in the development of their story and for various historical reasons, gradually began to interpret Christ's death on the cross and the eucharistic remembrance of him as a sacrifice, [22] this interpretation was wrought with difficulties and ancient cultic overlays. Certainly today the understanding of atonement and restitution demanded by an offended deity because of a sin committed by the first human has little if any viability. God demanding a human sacrifice, or Jesus taking on our sins and offering to die on the cross for us in expiation for them, also does not seem plausible upon thoughtful reflection on a divine–human relationship of love. How then can one understand sacrifice within a Christian perspective?

Robert J. Daly, citing Edward J. Kilmartin's work, *The Eucharist in the West: History and Theology*, offers the following explanation:

> Sacrifice in the New Testament understanding—and thus in its Christian understanding—is, in the first place, the self-offering of the Father in the gift of his Son, and in the second place the unique response of the Son in his humanity to the Father, and in the third place, the self-offering of believers in union with Christ by which they share in his covenant relation with the Father. . . . The radical self-offering of the faithful is the only spiritual response that constitutes an authentic sacrificial act according to the New Testament (Romans 12:1). [23]

Although God pervades and empowers all of creation, in Jesus, God comes to expression in the fullness of divinity in human form and awakens human consciousness to this divine self-revelation and self-gift. In turn, this divine self-expression is not passively received by Jesus but is responded to out of the fullness of his being. As mentioned earlier, his food is to be about God's will: to bring to completion in his own life humanity's continued self-offering to God. In the third "place," then, and by the power of God's Spirit, the faithful followers of Jesus offer themselves to God in the eucharist; and with the heartfelt commitment of their "Amen," spoken at the eucharistic meal, they are *transubstantiated*, and they become the Body of Christ.

The symbols[24] of bread and wine speak powerfully of the totality, the intensity, if you will, of what is happening here. The assembly gathers to receive the sacred species. They receive the bread, broken and *shared*. All partake of the same loaf[25] and in the eating become one with each other and with Christ who gives himself that way—gathering all together as his Mystical Body in their commitment to the new covenant. As the assembly drinks of the cup, the wine, symbol of Christ's blood (flowing through and giving life and energy, as it did, to every cell of his body), also empowers and flows through the faithful and, in turn, strengthens them in the self-offering to which, as Christians, they are devoting their lives.

In order to gain a full appreciation of what it means to "be the Body," as Saint Augustine admonishes us—referring to our response when we receive the eucharistic symbols[26]—it is essential that Christians of today reclaim their *active* role in the eucharistic celebration. It seems to me that there is still too much passivity among the faithful of today, and often not even an awareness of their own call to authentic self-offering. As mentioned before, it has been claimed since 1208 CE that the priest, by the power of his office, is the only one who can "celebrate Mass." It is reassuring, therefore to return once more to the observations of Robert J. Daly:

> The assembly, in words solemnly proclaimed by the presider, prays that the Holy Spirit come and sanctify

these gifts and make them become for us the body and blood of Christ. Thus, *it is not the presider who conse-crates*. The presider, speaking solemnly in the name of the assembly, prays that the Holy Spirit consecrate the gifts and also consecrate us, the assembly, so that we may become the true Body of Christ offering ourselves with Jesus (for the force of this prayer is to make us one with and part of Jesus' self-offering) to God.[27]

What is significant here is that the priest is not, nor does he need to be, a mediator between Christ and the assembly; "the role of the priest is embedded in the Christ/Church relationship that brings about the Eucharist."[28] What needs to be reclaimed is the *recognition* that the one acting and speaking is the *local assembly*. It is the assembly, led by the presider, who prays the eucharistic prayer. There is no place here for passivity. "The Church in supreme confidence—it knows it is the Body of Christ, indeed the Bride of Christ—asks God . . . to send [God's] spirit to sanctify the eucharistic gifts and the eucharistic assembly, in order to make them, together, the true Body of Christ."[29]

At eucharist, then, there are two events that happen through the working of God's Spirit. The bread and wine become the body and blood of Christ, and the members of the assembly become more fully the Body of Christ, which they already are by virtue of their baptism. There is, of course, no visible change. The bread and wine retain their appearance and effects. Reference to the assembly as Christ's Body is clearly symbolic. The effects will ultimately be visible only in the way we live our lives and embrace the new covenant into which we were baptized, and to which, once again at this eucharistic meal, we have committed ourselves. *And it is the latter transformation that takes precedence here.*

For many years now, we have lived with what might perhaps best be called a theology of "objectification," where the words of consecration uttered over the eucharistic elements and their subsequent transubstantiation were of primary concern—the central event of the eucharistic celebration. This theology saw the priest-presider as *the* central agent who alone, by virtue of an "ontological change" brought about at his ordination, could "mediate" the divine event in memory of Jesus's last meal with his disciples and centered on the elements of bread and wine. In the light of this, the theology proposed above can be quite puzzling and perhaps upsetting. Here, however, is how Robert J. Daly, well versed on this topic, addresses this issue:

> That the eucharistic elements become the body and blood of Christ is not an end in itself. The final purpose of eucharistic transformation is not the eucharistic body of Christ become present on this or that altar. *This happens for us, that we may become more fully and more truly the Body of Christ.* Eucharistic real presence exists not for its own sake—it is not happening just so that the body of Christ can be found on this or that altar—*but for the purpose of the eschatological transformation of the participants.* Take that away and Eucharist becomes (even blasphemously) meaningless. . . . [I]f the transformation of the eucharistic elements is not having its effects in the virtuous dispositions of the participants, *if the participants are not at least beginning to be transformed, at least beginning to appropriate the self-offering virtuous dispositions of Christ, then there is no eucharistic presence.*[30]

Nothing, in my estimation, can be more direct and challenging. A lengthy theological discussion about which theologian of note, especially in our church's two thousand years of dogmatizing and discussing, agrees or disagrees with this position is not my intention here, nor of primary interest.

It is clear that many of today's educated laity no longer come together for their Sunday duty to celebrate eucharist simply in order to passively witness the consecration of bread and wine. It seems that if they experience that this is what is expected of them, they often simply stop attending.[31] The medieval practice of running from church to church in order to obtain the grace of gazing at the consecrated host lifted up by the presider as the bells ring has definitely been left behind. Prayer, and certainly the central prayer of the church, is for *our* transformation. This means that it is for our appropriating into our lives and embracing the self-giving love of Christ. Eucharist celebrates our response to the totally loving, totally free gift of God's self in Christ. It is our "yes," our "me too"—in spite of our poverty and sinfulness. It is the "Amen" that responds to the tenderness that invites us to enter into the loving and deeply personal life of God. We come together to grow together into the authenticity of our "Amen" through the power of God's Spirit.

Sacrifice in its Latin root means "to make holy." The event of transformation that is experienced during eucharistic consecration is indeed very holy. But without *our* self-giving response to this sacred moment, without *our being re-membered into it*, even if it takes a lifetime of growing, what would its purpose be? Perhaps to soften this rather blunt question somewhat, it would help to reflect on how Edward Schillebeeckx addresses the contemporary shift from a primarily "object" and definition-oriented approach to the eucharist back to the earlier celebration of eucharistic presence in the community of the post-resurrection Jesus movement:

In the new approach to the distinctively eucharistic presence of Christ, an attempt is made above all to situate this presence within the sphere of Christ's real presence within the believer and in the whole believing community. In this way the early Christian view can be recovered in its full dimensions—the distinctively eucharistic presence is directed towards bringing about Christ's more intimate presence in each individual believer and in the community of believers as a whole. The eucharistic presence is thus no longer isolated. We no longer say, "Christ is there," without asking for whom he is present.[32]

The "for whom?" question is clearly of primary importance to move us away from the personal detachment that so easily can set in with an overemphasis on the sacred species "out there on the altar." Schillebeeckx cites P. Schoonenberg's reflection in *Verbum* 26 (1959) to reassure those who find the shift from what we used to understand by the "Real Presence" to a broader and more personal understanding somewhat challenging or even disconcerting: "Those among us who are older rightly regard their faith in Christ's presence under the species as a great treasure. This treasure is not taken away from them when . . . this presence of Christ under the species is situated entirely within his presence in the community."[33] What is important to remember is that the original orientation and emphasis of the earliest Christian community gatherings for eucharist was not on interpretation and definitions, on objective "out there" reality, but on *experience* and *celebration*.

Perhaps it would help to summarize succinctly and simply what is intended and what is happening as we gather for the breaking of the bread and the sharing of the cup in memory of and in commitment to the covenant of love and justice envisioned by Jesus before his crucifixion and death. We believe that in this celebration of remembrance Christ gives himself to us under the appearance of bread and wine—a meal. Bread and wine become the bearers of Christ's gift of himself to us and to God. We in turn as members of Christ's Body—his church—offer ourselves to God in Christ, and do so with our lives. In this way each moment of our daily living can become a "eucharistic" event as, in Christ, we give ourselves in compassion and care to one another.

Reflection

A beautiful experience that illustrates most poignantly this continuous eucharistic self-gift was shared with me not long ago by one of my friends who ministers as chaplain in the county jail of Los Angeles. I include her experience here with her permission as a powerful example of the eucharistic mystery that calls all of us to be Christ's Body and to share ourselves with one another:

> One morning during early community Eucharist, I found myself distracted and bored. When I realized this, I prayed, "Dear God, awaken me to what is happening here."
>
> I simply could not conjure up any feeling, connection, or response to the ceremony going on before me. Leaving the chapel, I felt it would have been better had I not attended.
>
> Later that day I was conducting a tour in the punishment unit of the county jail. This area is called the "hole" because it is in the basement of the building with pipes running along the ceiling and with only a 25-watt bulb barely lighting each confined cell. Inmates are allowed nothing whatsoever except a Bible, which they can hardly read in the semi-darkness. Food trays are left in an opened slot in the door when meals are delivered. Confinement can last anywhere from two weeks to a year, depending on the behavior of the person and the background of the case. In time, one of two things can happen, depending on the personality: the person will adjust and find the solitude bearable or he or she will revert to extreme depression and withdrawal.

As I was walking the halls and listening to the yells or babbles or expletives being shouted and echoed off the concrete walls, I suddenly heard a frightened little voice of what could only be a young woman calling out, "Chaplain! Chaplain! Please help me!" When I turned back, I saw that a little hand was sticking out of one of the slots gesturing for me to come. I knelt before the door and the hand grabbed mine and held on as if she were sinking. Tears exploded from the dark cell as she poured out her heart, her fears, her confusion. It seemed that the FBI wanted her isolated until her case was investigated, and the "hole" was the only place to put her.

I bent to see her face, tear-stained and trembling, and gazed upon her hand clinging to mine, and suddenly I said to myself, "This is Eucharist! This is my body given over for you! Take it!" Was she receiving me, or was I receiving her? The mystery of it left me stunned, and I suddenly realized that my morning prayer was being answered.

Several weeks later as I was visiting a general floor, a young inmate called me over and with a big smile informed me that she was the one I had visited in the "hole." She said, "Your presence and touch gave me the strength I needed to become calm and peaceful for the rest of the time I had to spend there."

What is the mystery we are so privileged to enter into each time we receive Eucharist? What is the dynamic poured into our being that becomes the Christed presence in our world? What form does Eucharist take as we go about our daily routines? Why did I need a broken little girl, an outcast in the dark "hole" of the county jail, to remind me that Jesus was calling us both to sit at the banquet and be fed by each other?

S. Catherine Marie Bazaar, O.P.

Thoughts and Questions for Meditation

1. What are your thoughts about Robert Mickens's "Letter from Rome"? Can you understand it as a description of eucharist? Why or why not?

2. Do you believe that we need to retrieve the primacy of meal in our understanding of eucharist? If so, how might this change our celebration?

3. What are your favorite New Testament stories about the mercy, inclusivity, and forgiveness modeled by Jesus?

4. Do you believe it is true that love and unconditional acceptance bring about conversion much more readily than judgment, condemnation, and exclusion? If so, why?

5. Do you agree that leadership is enhanced when one has a deep down sense of one's own brokenness and personal need for mercy and healing?

6. What is your reaction to John Dominic Crossan's view of the "bread-and-fish Eucharist"? Were you surprised? Can you see its relevance to the main eucharistic purpose?

7. The Last Supper, according to Bernard Cooke and others, was not the occasion for the first ordination to the priesthood nor for the establishment of an official eucharistic ritual. Both developed over time. Is this surprising to you? If so, why?

8. If the emphasis during the eucharistic meal was on action, never merely on words, what action do we need to look for and live out in order for the eucharist to be life-giving and effective for us?

9. How do you react to Robert J. Daly's threefold aspects of the New Testament understanding of sacrifice? What does he mean by "the self-offering of the Father in the gift of his Son"? Also, how do his observations concerning who, in fact "consecrates" affect you?

10. Does the assembly to which you belong recognize its obligation to be about the eucharistic prayer and become "more fully the Body of Christ which they already are"?
11. What are the two transformations that need to take place at eucharist? And which one takes precedence?
12. What is your response to the following observation: "But without *our* self-giving response to this sacred moment (eucharistic consecration), without *our being re-membered into it*, even if it takes a lifetime of growing, what would its purpose be?
13. What is your response to the questions S. Catherine Marie Bazaar asked herself at the end of her reflection? Have you had similar questions that do not yield easily to an answer but need to be pondered for a long time and then be allowed to bear fruit in our daily lives?

I Know That My Redeemer Lives

Light Showings

The Rain Puddle

I am alone this Saturday morning. Outside the light is soft. Snow still blankets the earth and sound is lost in silence. Before, when the sky was dark and not nearly day, the picture was given to me. I saw a rain puddle and in it were reflected the yellows, peaches, and pinks of sunrise. In an ordinary puddle, the colors of sunrise shine softly on any street, rut or path—anywhere in the world.

I see within this common rain puddle *all* the colors of heaven shining. . . . As the great sun rises on any city street or rutted dirt road, in schoolyard or in forest, in the jungle or in any path in the world, heaven shines.

Why do we have so many, long tiresome books thinking it out, insisting that heaven, that spirit, that God must be experienced this way or that way, only directly available to these people or those, or some future time?

I do not believe God can be dissected or boxed in by our tiny thoughts, or only found in past writings of centuries ago. Heaven is with us now.

Look into any common rain puddle anywhere on our earth when the sun shines on it. You will see God's light.

Whoever you are in this life, a rain puddle is here for you. It shines with all the colors of this new day, the day that has opened for each of us here and now.[1]

Nancy Heuck Johanson

If Christ Has Not Been Raised, Our Faith is in Vain

I started my reflections on the eucharist in the previous chapter with Robert Mickens's "Letter from Rome" and his account of the daily welcoming banquet for Rome's poor at Sant'Eustachio's—a museum church in Rome. I ended the chapter with S. Catherine Marie Bazaar's reflection on her encounter with a young woman inmate in the "hole" of the Los Angeles county jail. These stories clearly are eucharistic in a most authentic way, and, because of this, they also bear witness to the resurrection, to Christ's living presence among us still. They speak of the power of love that can give life where death seems to dominate, that can offer hope where despair seems inevitable, that can bestow dignity where humiliation and oppression seem victorious. They touch the heart, but they also do so much more! They are strong, they are true, they are alive, and, above all, they speak of *presence:* the presence that is proclaimed in our "Amen" as the living Body of the Holy One with us always, as the power of the resurrection manifest in our very midst. Finally, these stories in their simplicity and straightforwardness speak to our deepest self since what is revealed in them is what we all, knowingly or not, yearn for. They are strong and they are true precisely because they point us to our sacred covenant as baptized into the life of Christ, as called to be his living presence in this world and in our time.

Eucharist, the shared meal, is the charter event of Christianity-*lived*. It is where *presence* happens. But it happens only in the *sharing*. We recognize Christ *there*. His life in us is meant to be given away. Eucharist cannot be held on to, dispensed frugally, and only under certain conditions. It is not meant to be a reward for those deemed worthy and denied to those who are not. It is there for all who hunger and thirst. Prodigality without need for an apology, for contrition and penance are its hallmark. The parable in Luke 15:20, 22 makes this very clear, as do the post-resurrection "eucharists" of the disciples in Jerusalem and at the seashore in Galilee where apologies and repentance would certainly have been fitting but were *never* demanded. He died for this vision of God's forgiving, inclusive, nonjudgmental, nonviolent reign, and he rises in each of us over and over again every time we proclaim it with our lives. "Christ does not read the Bible, the New Testament, or the Gospel. He is the *norm* of the Bible, the *criterion* of the New Testament, the *incarnation* of the Gospel. . . . The *person*, not the book, and the *life*, not the text, are decisive and constitutive for us."[2] Forgiveness, prodigality, healing, acceptance, sharing!

Reflection

Paul, in his First Letter to the Corinthians 15:14, insists that "if Christ has not been raised . . . [our] faith is in vain." It would have no purpose, be of no avail, pointless, futile, fruitless.

There are a variety of interpretations of this Pauline conviction, but as I was meditating on it and on the power of the resurrection it proclaims, the challenge of the reverse possibility invaded my thoughts. I felt somewhat overpowered by this, especially in the light of so much that is surfacing today in our world and is demanding our attention. I forced myself, however, with some tangible reluctance, to consider and now also to invite the reader to ponder the converse of Paul's declaration:

Given what we have claimed Jesus was *really* about—what he *lived for* and *died for*,

- What if we, as Christians, really do not truly embrace his vision and therefore give it no serious credence?
- What if our lives do not bear witness, therefore, to the all inclusive love of Christ, and the "energy" of his resurrection is nowhere visible?
- What if we proclaim ourselves to be his followers, to walk in his footsteps, but no one would know or even care?
- What if the world, as almost one-third "Christian," is in fact not a better, a more compassionate, a more neighbor-centered and healing place?

What would then be the meaning of the resurrection? What would be its point, its *why*?

What if our faith as manifest in our lives really has no purpose, is fruitless, "in vain"? What if in our society (where on our dollar bills we claim "In God We Trust"),

- the hungry are still starving,
- the homeless in increasing numbers are still roaming the streets at night looking for shelter and warmth,
- the poor cannot earn a living wage,
- women, as well as their children, are raped—often without genuine recourse,
- the destitute are sold into slavery, trafficked throughout the "civilized" world, with little or no regard for their freedom and dignity, and with little if any legal protection,

- widespread exclusion because of race, sexual orientation, gender, language, culture, and even religion still prevails?

What, in such a society, would be the point of the resurrection? How could we explain why God raised, why God vindicated, Christ Jesus? Who would be paying attention? Whose lives would be affected by this vindication?

These questions are jarring, disturbing, and painful for any of us who want to take our faith seriously and live it. These themes are not new for this book. We have pondered similar questions in the previous chapters when, for example, we reflected on the Christmas parables, or when in chapter 4 we also wondered whether the world is indeed a better place because of Christianity. Statistics show the number of Christians at 31.5 percent of the world's population. What visible sign of our Christian heritage do we have to show for it?

I do not believe that giving in to self-righteous indignation at what these questions suggest is helpful here. The reality of the world situation and what I would call our global disease of selfishness can simply not be ignored that way. We are all called to be our brothers' and sisters' keepers, and we *are that* with more responsibility than ever before because, as we discussed in chapter 4, today we *know* that we are held in cosmic interconnectedness with all of reality. Nothing we do, not even a single thought we have, goes without either healing or destructive repercussions. Perhaps a humble trust in God's mercy and in God's patience with all of us, including our religious establishments and governments, is first and foremost what all of us should pray for.

In this chapter, our theme question probes into the meaning of the resurrection and the energy it unleashed. How, as Christ's church, have we been infused by it? To what tangible change in terms of this energy can we point, can we commit ourselves? Or is it conceivable that the reality of Christ's rising has for many of us simply become an "icon" of our faith, nothing more—something we celebrate at Easter and then forget for the rest of the year after the Easter season is over? My hope is that some reflection on the Easter event and its implications can help focus for us the profound and challenging gift of our Christian heritage.

A Developing Tradition

How were the followers of Jesus affected by their encounter with the living presence of Christ after the crucifixion? How was their vision and their behavior changed, enhanced, and expanded after the events of his death and burial opened up to unexpected encounters with his living presence? An obvious and quick answer originating in our personal expectations most likely would be: "completely." They were totally changed, delighted, amazed, awed, perhaps also somewhat afraid until he put them at ease. All in all, we would expect that they must have had extraordinary and overwhelming experiences that eventually moved them into action, having totally transformed them. In some respects these conjectures are certainly true. We read about them toward the end of the Gospels, in the Acts of the Apostles, and also in the letters of Paul and the other writers. We cannot forget, however, what was discussed in chapter 2, namely, that some statements and stories in scripture are true but do not necessarily need to be factual. They clearly are not simple fabrications. Rather, they have a truth-value beyond the empirical at a much deeper than factual level.

Many of us, living at this time in history, may have been accustomed to approach the post-resurrection accounts much like other reports we hear and read about in the news media, namely, factually, and as happening in the order in which they are presented. Perhaps, what we tend to forget, or do not expect, is that the stories of our faith were written *in the light of faith*. They were written as faith events that were transmitted for us, so that we also might believe. They were not written for the purpose of accurately and objectively conveying occurrences that happened sequentially. Even though we often talk about them and listen to homilies about them as if they had been reported by witnesses who could take an oath as to their accuracy, they, as so many stories in scripture, describe the Easter event symbolically. The reason for this quite simply was largely because what happened at Easter was *beyond* description, *beyond* ordinary experience, and could not be formulated in any other way. That something happened to the Jesus community after his death seems beyond doubt. That parabolic accounts seem to have been the only vehicle for speaking about the experience of life and vindication makes whatever the resurrection means not less important but important on a much deeper, transcendent level.

The post-resurrection experiences with the Risen One need, therefore, to be understood as beyond purely natural, physical, and temporal reality. They cannot be classified as historical in the normal use of that word and might, as McBrien suggests, best be spoken of as "trans-historical."[3] Once again, they were written in their particular style, not to deceive but simply because what happened was beyond factual reporting and could only be described symbolically. Roger Haight, in his recent book *Spirituality Seeking Theology,* explains this well. He maintains that "spiritual language about transcendent reality is *necessarily* symbolic," and then clarifies that "the term 'symbol' as it is used here represents a strong vehicle of communicating transcendent truths that cannot be expressed in any other way. These stories are like sacraments that represent and mediate spiritual truths through the concrete images used in description and narrative."[4]

The Gospels generally, then, need to be approached as good news *for us to embrace and live.* Exegetes tell us that they were written many years after Jesus of Nazareth walked this earth—some 35 to 60 years or more. They, and certainly

the resurrection accounts, were written about real people
who had lived through an encounter of profound grace, at
times understood and appreciated and, at other times, not.
They had suffered loss and pain and despair, and then were
once again lifted up in unexpected ways. They had to make
sense out of all this. The written accounts were formulated
largely in and for communities as the immensity and depth of
what had been experienced began to sink in, and after many
attempts at understanding, many conversations, struggles,
doubts, moments of despair, and also some consolations and
eventual enlightenment. Clearly this would have taken time
and struggle. The late scripture scholar Marcus Borg says it
well when he explains that "Seeing the gospels as a developing tradition means that they are not primarily concerned
with historical reporting. Rather, *the gospels combine memory and testimony.* . . . They combine memory and witness,
memory and proclamation, memory and conviction. They
contain the communities' memories of the pre-Easter Jesus
and their post-Easter proclamation of his significance. They
combine Jesus remembered and Jesus proclaimed."[5] And it
is *this* Jesus—the human Jesus who lived among us and the
glorified and vindicated Christ—whom we have been called
to follow. It is *his* vision embraced and lived that makes us
truly Christian.

Given the approximate time of authorship and the prob-
able illiteracy of his immediate followers, it seems clear that
the Gospel accounts were not written by the first disciples
of Jesus, or by those who actually witnessed his death and
then were the first to experience him as alive and with them
still. One account of experiencing the living Christ that can,
however, most closely approximate the factual is that of
Paul's conversion, an experience that he mentions himself
(1 Cor. 15:3-8; Gal. 1:11-16), and that is also referred to
in Acts 9:13-19 and, again with some slight differences, in
Acts 22:6-21. The other post-resurrection experiences were
recorded many years later in parabolic form that mentions no

witnesses to the actual resurrection event as such and gives no description of what precisely happened. What we have, instead, are accounts of encounters, first with what appear to be otherworldly beings—angels in dazzling clothes—at the empty tomb who speak of his having been raised, and later of experiences with the risen Christ himself.

In the light of what was discussed above about these events as transhistorical, the absence of firsthand reports of an actual physical resurrection should not, however, diminish what is written in the Gospels. As Haight, once again, explains, "The resurrection should be understood not as an empirical event of history but precisely as *Jesus being drawn into the life of God*, the infinite and transcendent one. Resurrection is not a historical event but a transcendent event."[6] It was proclaimed as a testament to the living Christ, that what he proclaimed is of God; that death does not have the final say; that he is held in God; and that his living presence gives hope to all people of good will. "When [the Easter experiences as reported] are taken too literally as descriptive of historical events as they happened, they become a trap that . . . radically limits the range of religious experience and the meaning of resurrection itself. Literalism reduces the Easter experience of Jesus' resurrection to naïve religious stories."[7]

If what has been discussed so far concerning the historicity of the Easter events discourages or disappoints some readers, it may help to consider what resurrection, understood merely as physical resuscitation, would mean. If we consider John's account of the raising of Lazarus back to life, we will have to accept the fact that this would have to be understood as a temporal, earthly event and not an entrance into eternal life. What this implies, therefore, is that Lazarus, visible to all and living once again with his sisters, would have to die again at some time in the future. John's account here clearly does not refer to a resurrection, as did the Easter stories. John (12:10) in fact mentions a plot by the chief priests to kill Lazarus again since, because of his having been raised from the dead, more

and more people were beginning to believe in Jesus. The resurrection of Jesus, then, was more than resuscitation, and the
appearance narratives need to be understood at a *deeper level*
than simply having Jesus back alive and with his disciples.

Hans Küng speaks to this deeper level beautifully when
he first clarifies that "the resurrection just does not mean a
return to this life in space and time. Death is not canceled,
but definitely conquered. Neither does it mean a continuation of this life in space and time. The very expression 'after
death' is misleading; eternity is not characterized by 'before'
and 'after.'"[8] He then offers a powerful vision of how the
resurrection needs to be understood:

> *"Resurrection" means* a life that bursts through the
> dimensions of space and time in God's invisible, imper-
> ishable, incomprehensible domain. *This is what is meant
> by "heaven"—not the heaven of the astronauts, but God's
> heaven. It means going into reality, not going out.*
>
> Resurrection therefore means positively that Jesus
> did not die into nothingness, but in death and from
> death died into that incomprehensible and comprehen-
> sive absolutely last/absolutely first reality, was indeed
> taken up by that most real reality, which we designate
> by the name of God. And it is this very act that the
> first witnesses regard as having universal importance, as
> having importance also for [us].[9]

Richard McBrien also addresses the deeper level necessary
for an authentic religious understanding of the resurrection
in contemporary times when he insists that "Christian theology today, in keeping with the results of modern New Testament studies, more commonly understands the resurrection
as central to, not simply confirmatory of, Christian faith, and
as the beginning, not simply the end, of the story."[10] An earlier, somewhat incomplete understanding of the resurrection
event would have seen it simply as vindication by God: an

affirmation of divine favor and of Jesus's life and message as truly from God. I believe that this interpretation is certainly true and in fact very important even if incomplete, and that it does not have to be rejected, though I would want to see it expanded. In its incompleteness it could give the impression that the vindication is indeed *the end* of the Jesus event: He came, he proclaimed his message, he was rejected and killed, but God raised him and declared in that way that his message was in fact true. If we then were to add to this interpretation the traditional belief that Jesus, in accordance to God's will, also atoned for our sins by his crucifixion and death and in this way opened for us the gates of heaven which had been closed to us because of Adam's sin, then *there truly would be finality.* But at what cost?

The conclusion could then be drawn that, to put it somewhat crudely, given Christ's atonement, our difficulties have been taken care of. We are redeemed, privileged, and the easiest response would be to say "thank you," observe the standard requirements including church attendance on Sundays, but otherwise simply move on with our baptismal certificate tucked safely away somewhere with all the other papers one might need for identification. Somehow, even though gratitude is certainly called for, this kind of a response seems banal, trite, clearly superficial, and much too simplistic for serious religious reflection and consequent behavior. It should not satisfy anyone who takes her or his life as a Christian seriously. I cannot help wondering, though, whether, as outlandish as it may appear to some, it is that uncommon.

Reflection

I live in a city not too different from other large western cities. One of its major concerns at the moment is to work at refurbishing its center. The inner city, with an attractive waterfront and some lovely old buildings including beautiful churches, has become a major interest for the upwardly mobile population who, after years of living in the suburbs, are now attracted to the opportunities (a casino, bars, dog parks, upscale shopping) that developers are working hard to provide in the process of gentrification. The "problem," as in most of our cities, is the presence of numerous homeless and destitute men, women, and children, who for many years have found some refuge where now the wealthy want to live. My city has therefore decided simply to displace "these people," to move them away to less conspicuous and certainly less desirable areas and generally to deny their presence as members of the community—make them "invisible," in other words. Recognizing and admitting their homelessness and providing a place for them to live where they, in fact, for many years have formed community, where some try desperately to find available work, albeit at below subsistence wages, and where low-cost transportation and some food pantries are available for them, seem a Christ-like alternative that appears never to have been considered.

The percentage of Catholics alone in my city is 26.04 percent of the total population—higher by far than any other Christian denomination. It is the center of an archdiocese with a beautiful cathedral and a $400,000 mansion in the suburbs for its archbishop. Could it be that for many Catholics of my city, the notion that "being saved," believing what we are told to believe, going to Mass and saying our prayers is sufficient, and that the rest is best left to others, our elected, also often "Christian" representatives?

But the Christian faith is meant to be lived and has nothing to do with finality as such. The Easter event marked its beginning *not its end.*

Christ's vindication initiated our resurrection faith as a new way of being. What Jesus taught and proclaimed were not theories or dry propositions. He modeled a way of life, and it was *that life—for us to live*—that was vindicated by God.

His identification of God's cause with [ours], God's will with the general well-being of [humankind] was therefore right. . . . He was right too in identifying himself with the weak, sick, poor, underprivileged, even with the moral failures, the irreligious and godless. And his plea for pardon instead of punishment was right. . . . Finally and above all he was right in the commitment of his life, in his perseverance and in continuing his way to the end.[11]

A theology of atonement suggesting a sacrificial death in restitution for a sin committed by the first human and inherited by us, thus afflicting us with depravity, a theology that justifies terrible cruelty toward an innocent victim and presents a perverted view of a Father God, seems to have done very little to bring about societal "redemption," transformation, a just and merciful society. It belongs to another era, and certainly should no longer be part of our religious self-understanding. This interpretation was acceptable at a time when cultic sacrifices to appease or flatter the gods were part of religious practice. They were expected and demanded of all citizens in Roman society, no matter what their belief, in order to prevent the various disasters gods could send if displeased with humanity. As Herbert Haag discusses, Christians in Roman society felt increasingly pressured, therefore, to interpret their eucharist in sacrificial terms.[12] Understanding sacrifice to an offended deity as "atonement for sin" became part of the enculturation of Jewish Christianity into the gentile world. The crucifixion of Jesus was seen as such an atonement and was explained as sacrifice along with eucharist as "an un-bloody sacrifice celebrated in remembrance."[13]

This context and those times, however, are no longer ours. Faith seeking understanding in the twenty-first century needs to move beyond interpretations that are no longer life-giving into a more time-relevant, creative, and responsible understanding of our precious heritage. I suggest that not doing so and neglecting to spend serious time prayerfully thinking through what Christ's mission really means for us today can open us up to serious abuse. Authentic Christianity is a tough religion. It makes demands on those who are baptized into its vision. Our faith, however, can easily become useless and even scandalous if we ignore the vision Christ's resurrection offers us and succumb instead to the illusory "finality" of Christ's death as atonement.

I wonder, for example,

- whether much of the condemnation and exclusion, as well as the discrimination that is practiced in various Christian denominations including my own church;
- whether the heartlessness we exhibit toward those we deem unworthy,
- the greed exhibited in some of our churches and dioceses,
- as well as the opulence in some ecclesial venues often paid for by others,
- and the indifference to just salaries for lay employees in many of our dioceses

may not have something to do with our thoughtless triumphalism dating back to bygone times of ecclesial princedoms and temporal power. It seems to me that all of this has nothing to do with the vision of Jesus.

And in our society,

- is the indifference to honesty,
- the addiction to greed, and
- our disregard for the poor (who should be "pulling themselves up by their own boot straps");
- is the ready use of war and torture against our enemies advocated by many who claim Christianity as their religion;
- is our hatred of those who are different, be it by race, or culture, or religion, or gender, or sexual orientation;

are all these and still many more atrocious violations of our baptismal commitment perhaps somehow related to that "artificial" *finality* that guarantees our salvation as long as we "claim" Jesus as our savior and follow the rules?

I suppose one might want to ask: savior from what? "From hell hereafter" is a worn-out answer and belongs only to all those who ignore the "hell" we all help create for one another and for ourselves right here on earth when we ignore the resurrection and its message. If our faith is in vain, if it is hollow, useless, fruitless, banal, cheap, and offers little hope, what is the point of the resurrection?

I feel a deep inner ache as I write this, for I cannot help remembering a poem by e.e. cummings that a friend of mine shared with me many years ago. It has no title and points simply to a timeless moment, a moment lost in the eternity of life when the poet, while walking in the dark, encounters the Christ. He experiences intense closeness—perhaps even intimacy—but finds in Christ nothing except utter (perhaps even heartbreaking) loneliness.

A Living Faith

What then can we truly say about Christ alive and among us? Perhaps it would be helpful to refer back to what we already discussed, namely, that the stories about the resurrection event were symbolic ways of speaking about a life-transforming experience that defied ordinary descriptive language. The accounts of the encounters with the Risen One were ways of speaking

1. about his living presence in the midst of his followers
2. of his abiding, transforming, and real influence experienced through the years that followed his death
3. about the vindication of the way of life that he had modeled and proclaimed, and

4. of the image of God as a loving and compassionate parent that he had invited all of us to embrace.

> Jesus' message, in the many ways it was delivered, [while he was on earth] stressed the goodness of God. It spoke of and dramatized God's loving and saving intent; it underlined the fidelity of God. Through his parables, those he told and the symbolic actions he performed, Jesus represented God's faithful commitment to the flourishing and fulfillment of human existence.[14]

The energy and power of conviction he radiated elicited in others the desire to follow him, to listen to his teachings, and accept his authority. It was *this* authority that "caused his disciples to remember him. And this memory of him is precisely what urged the disciples to experience *his* resurrection,"[15] and hope for and believe in their own. They proclaimed it, as well as their belief in the loving and life-giving parent God to whom Jesus had born witness throughout his life.

We can say then that the accounts of the resurrection event expressed the Christian faith as it *developed* after the death and burial of Jesus in the light of the experiences of his living and aiding presence in the early community of believers. Faith certainly was there among his followers during the life of Jesus with them as well, but the resurrection experience witnessed to the "continuation of divine empowerment through Jesus," which, as Crossan sees it, "developed, and widened across time and space after his execution. . . . It is precisely that *continued* experience of the [reign] of God as strengthened rather than weakened by Jesus' death that is Christian or Easter faith."[16] In his reflection on the resurrection experience, Crossan observes how the followers of Jesus during his life among them had gone forth in his name to heal, and had modeled open table fellowship. It would have been understandable, he suggests, if out of fear and discouragement after his crucifixion they had discontinued much of what they had done as his disciples prior to his death; if they had somehow "lost their faith," so to speak. But did this happen?

> Or, if they found themselves just as empowered as before, *was he not somehow still with them,* and how could that absent presence best be explained? The *Gospel of Thomas,* for example, uses only one title for Jesus. He is "the Living Jesus," who acts yesterday, today, and tomorrow as the Wisdom of God here on earth, and his missionaries participate in the divine Wisdom *by how they live, not just by how they talk.* They do not speak of resurrection but of unbroken and abiding presence.[17]

In the Jesus community, as well as in an ever-larger movement that formed after the death of Jesus, the experience of the resurrection, as McBrien explains, eventually moved from descriptions of what Jesus had done to prayer and worship, then to specifications as to what it means to be a Christian, and, finally, over the years, to explorations into the inner reality of Jesus Christ, that is, into theological speculations, into "his person, his natures and their relationships."[18] This clearly did not happen quickly and took place as Christianity expanded within other cultural settings (certainly and primarily in the Greco-Roman environment and its propensity for metaphysics). But this development was possible only, says McBrien, because of the early church's faith in the resurrection and the abiding presence and wisdom of Christ that enabled it

> to acknowledge the *divinity* of Jesus. And once the Church acknowledged the divinity of Jesus, it began laying the foundations for the doctrine of the *incarnation,* which sees Jesus as the Word made flesh (John 1:14). From the doctrine of the incarnation the Church was led ineluctably to the *preexistence* of Jesus (John

1:1; Philippians 2:5-9) and the question of his relationship to the whole of *creation* and the *history of salvation*
(Colossians 1:15-20; Romans 8:19-22; Ephesians 1:9-
10, 22, 23).[19]

As these scriptural references clearly indicate, however,
none of this was a smooth and progressive development. It
took, as was mentioned already, many years and struggles,
church councils, and often disagreements and the subsequent
condemnation of heretics to elucidate what had initially been
*a depth experience of the living presence of Christ's energy in the
midst of his followers; a presence that had empowered them to
continue to proclaim his message of compassion and love, and to
model it with their lives.*
I would suggest that creedal and complicated metaphysical formulations of divine personhood, preexistence, and
divine/human natures were intuited, at best if at all, only by
some of the more educated members of the very early church.
Very likely, they initially were not even thought about. The
Gospel of John, written sometime at the end of the first century, is perhaps the closest to these metaphysical concepts
but is distanced from the Easter events by almost sixty or
so years. This, of course, does not mean one should dismiss
as unimportant the metaphysical and theological attempts at
formulating the faith. It simply points to the long and arduous process of faith seeking understanding even from the earliest moments of Christianity.

And They Recognized Him
in the Breaking of the Bread

There is perhaps no scripture story more successful in illus-
trating the effort of "faith seeking understanding" in the
early Christian experiences after the resurrection than the
Emmaus story (Luke 24:13-35). As Roger Haight points

out, it allegorically offers us an account of "how the group of disciples, loosely but as a whole, came to the recognition over a more or less protracted period of time that Jesus was raised by God from death." He sees it as "depicting in very general but realistic terms stages through which the community would have moved to arrive at this conclusion of faith.[20]

The Emmaus story illustrates parabolically how for the followers of Jesus there had clearly been a time of deep loss after his crucifixion, a feeling of confusion, hopelessness, and horror at what had been so unexpected and so destructive of all they had anticipated and lived for. The disciples had desperately been trying to make sense of this. And then, Luke tells us in story form how, in the midst of their struggle, *Jesus had come to them and "walked" with them,* but initially had remained unrecognized. His presence, however, had moved them beyond their immediate concerns and inspired them to find connections they had not thought of before. He had brought "in-*spiration*," and their hearts had begun to burn with a sense of something more, with insights into deeper truth.

Luke's Emmaus account was meant to illustrate how, over time, their sharing and reflecting together had brought the disciples to see the underlying relation between the life and death of Jesus and the prophesies in the Hebrew scriptures, and how this ultimately became the basis for the Christian scriptures and the proclamation of the Good News.

Reflection

In the light of what has been discussed above, might not the question suggest to us today that

- if the Emmaus story (even though it tells of an event as if it unfolded on the evening of the resurrection) is really

intended to have us look at a much longer period of probing and searching and learning even into our day—assur-
ing us that the Risen One is ever with us and is present in
that very effort;

- if, indeed, this experience among the followers of Jesus is
  not an event that was factual/historical and needs rather
  to be understood metaphorically as an ongoing process of
  revelation, then

  1. What is there to stop us from thinking of this event as
     continuing on into an ever-deeper understanding and
     development of Christianity even beyond the revela-
     tions of the Christian scriptures that were clearly writ-
     ten within a particular time and culture and worldview?
  2. Why should God, who is beyond time and space, and
     why should the human spirit, ever longing for deeper
     understanding, be bound that way?
  3. Why could we not think of revelation as moving also
     into *our* day?
  4. Why, given what we in fact know today about the evolu-
     tion of consciousness, would we want to deny Christ's
     presence to human questing in our time, and restrict
     divine inspiration to the early church alone?
  5. Why should the presence of Christ Jesus, therefore, not
     be recognized also as he walks along the road with us
     who *today* feel compelled to make sense of our faith in
     the light of twenty-first-century discoveries that have
     altered our cosmology and continue to do so, allowing
     us to understand our place in the world in ever-new
     ways?

Marcus Borg responds quite directly to these questions:
"I think these kinds of experiences have continued among
Christians ever since,"[21] he says, and earlier in the same study
he observes, "Emmaus happens again and again."[22] Certainly
Teilhard de Chardin's experience of the Cosmic Christ, as
discussed in chapter 4, is a profound example of the ongoing

presence of the Living One in our midst. His writings offer passionate testimony to the relational power of love manifest throughout the universe. From atoms to self-aware humanity, all of creation is invited to communion in an ever-deeper embrace of love as, suffused by Christ's self-giving love, we move toward Christification—a living testament to his resurrected and living presence in our times.

Unfortunately, the sincere seekers of *our* time—those who continue to question and whose hearts also are burning with a sense of Emmaus presence—are often (as was Teilhard) faced with, and then try against all odds to move beyond, official ecclesial pronouncements. These are declared as permanent but often are based on what we know today to be clearly indefensible theories of bygone days. Finality is a human need based on our ingrained dualistic obsession with permanence and our fear of change. To impose it on thinkers and seekers who sincerely are given to the service of truth as it is emerging seems to me to be nothing other than an ill-advised attempt to shortchange revelation. Constructive dialogue is the only honest and indeed humble way to approach what presents itself to us as ever an open-ended process of unconcealment. Our evolving universe is suffused with the divine and is holy. It is a constantly emerging event of truth gifting the human spirit in whom it comes to consciousness. We honor that emergence when we accept that, given the consciousness with which we have been graced, we need to respond to it as we have been created to respond—namely, as ever searching, probing, and thinking. We betray our calling when we force finality on our quest out of an obsessive need for control.

For those who executed Jesus and who (their job being finished) then walked away, there was a naïve "finality" to all that happened on that day. For them, the troublemaker was dead. He was gone at last. Life could now go back to normal. Rules would be followed once again without questions, and those who wished to do otherwise would soon, at their peril, come to know better. I sense an illusory and death-dealing, cadaverous atmosphere surrounding expectations and absolutes such as these. But Jesus Christ proved them, and will continue to prove them, futile and false. *He is alive* and is with us "yesterday and today and forever." He is bound by no one, not by death-dealing finalities nor by absolute and also deadening declarations of certitude. As he did on the road to Emmaus, so today, he elicits discussion, conversation, searching, and questioning within or without official venues, because only the truth—as an evolving and ever-transforming process—will set us free. He urges us toward the *process of revelation* because without the searching and the questioning and the burning of our hearts, the ever-deepening and evolving quest for the living God is diminished and ultimately destroyed.

In the Emmaus allegory the disciples urge the "stranger" in their midst to stay with them when they arrive at their destination, and they ask him to share a meal with them. During their table fellowship, the Risen One, who had walked with them unrecognized throughout their long struggle toward understanding, is finally encountered. He is "known" in the breaking of the bread—a eucharistic event. They remember his promise of his abiding oneness with them, and they realize that, indeed, he was raised by God.

We too find him in the breaking of the bread. That is how he called all of us to remember him. The Risen One was encountered that way in almost all the post-resurrection parables. And to the present day, if our eucharist is celebrated with communal and personal commitment to transformation, it is the presencing of Christ. It is the celebration of his Body—*alive here and now*, and in each one of us as we go forth to live the resurrection wherever we are and in whatever we do. As the disciples knew him in the breaking of the bread and recognized him long ago—alive and present among them—so we also are called to know him today:

Christ yesterday and today, the *Alpha* and the *Omega,* the beginning and the end.

Eucharist and resurrection are one.

Thoughts and Questions for Meditation

1. How do your see the stories related by Robert Mickens and S. Catherine Marie Bazaar as both eucharistic experiences and as witnessing to the resurrection? Have you had similar experiences in your own life?

2. "Eucharist, the shared meal, is the charter event of Christianity-*lived.* It is where *presence* happens. But it happens only in the *sharing.* We recognize Christ *there.* His life in us is meant to be given away." What have you come to understand by this observation? Do you agree with it, or not? If so, why? If not, why not?

3. "Christ does not read the Bible, the New Testament, or the Gospel. He is the *norm* of the Bible, the *criterion* of the New Testament, the *incarnation* of the Gospel. . . . The *person*, not the book, and the *life*, not the text, are decisive and constitutive for us." How do you understand this claim by John Dominic Crossan?

4. The examples given to illustrate a faith that is "in vain" are not easy to face. What do you make of the question that, should these examples be true, what would be the purpose, the point, of the resurrection? How could we explain why God raised, why God vindicated, Christ Jesus? Who would be paying attention? Whose lives would be affected by this vindication?

5. How do you respond to the implication that resurrection, as physical resuscitation, needs to be replaced by a deeper understanding of presence that truly affects our lives?

6. Is it conceivable that the reality of Christ's rising has for many of us simply become an "icon" of our faith, nothing more—something we celebrate at Easter and then

forget for the rest of the year after the Easter season is over? If it is not, how do you see the resurrection influencing your life?

7. How do you relate to this chapter's discussion of the parabolic, allegorical nature of the resurrection stories? Does this make them less truth-worthy? Is the following observation of Roger Haight helpful to you? "The resurrection should be understood not as an empirical event of history but precisely as *Jesus being drawn into the life of God*, the infinite and transcendent one. Resurrection is not a historical event but a transcendent event."

8. How have you come to understand the claim of vindication with respect to God's raising Jesus from the dead? How is that related to the following statement that the Christian faith is meant to be lived and has nothing to do with finality as such? "The Easter event marked its beginning not its end. Christ's vindication initiated our resurrection faith as a new way of being."

9. "Authentic Christianity is a tough religion. It makes demands on those who are baptized into its vision. Our faith, however, can easily become useless and even scandalous if we ignore the vision Christ's resurrection offers us and succumb instead to the illusory 'finality' of Christ's death as atonement." What is your response to this statement?

10. In the light of the reflections offered in the section A Living Faith, how have you come to understand the resurrection experience? Are you comfortable with this interpretation? If so, why? If not, why not?

11. Can you accept the fact that "revelation" continues in our day? How do you understand this statement?

12. How do you see the connection between eucharist and resurrection? Are they one? What are the conditions that are necessary for this to be true?

What I Believe

I believe in God, the holy "Ground of being," divine source, suffusing all of creation with life, consciousness, and energy, and holding it in unconditional love.

I believe in Jesus the Christ in whom no less than the fullness of divinity is manifest. While with us in human form he modeled for us a life of compassion, inclusivity, unconditional forgiveness and mercy. He confronted unjust structures of oppression and selfishness, and encouraged us toward a community of sisterly and brotherly love.

He was crucified by the powers of domination, who could not abide his freedom and challenge. But God raised him, and he is with us still—empowering us to live the liberating vision of total and unrestricted love and compassion.

I believe in the divine Spirit who flows through us and helps us understand the life-giving presence of God.

I believe in Mary and Joseph, the parents of Jesus who nurtured him into maturity and who, in our day, along with the communion of saints—those who have departed this life—are our protectors, our guides, wisdom figures, and helpers in need.

As a member of the Catholic community, I believe in the Christian communion called to live the vision of Jesus.

I believe that upon my passing from this earthly existence, I will join the communion of the blessed and be taken deep into the heart of God.

To God be glory and praise forever.

Notes

1. On Living in a Time of Bridging

1. Miriam Therese Winter, Adair Lummis, Allison Stokes, *Defecting in Place: Women Claiming Responsibility for Their Own Lives* (New York: Crossroad, 1994), iii. This study concerned women primarily, but I would claim that today men also are "defecting in place."

2. Bernadette Farrell, *O God, You Search Me* (Portland, OR: OCP, 1992).

2. For Unto Us a Child Is Born, a Son Is Given (Isaiah 9:6)

1. John Dominic Crossan, *God and Empire: Jesus against Rome: Then and Now* (New York: HarperCollins, 2007), 28. Also, John Dominic Crossan and Jonathan L. Reed, *Excavating Jesus: Beneath the Stones, Behind the Text* (New York: HarperCollins, 2001), 87, 88.

2. Marcus J. Borg and John Dominic Crossan, *The First Christmas: What the Gospels Really Teach about Jesus's Birth* (New York: HarperCollins, 2007), 120–23.

3. Michael Peppard, *The Son of God in the Roman World* (New York: Oxford University Press, 2011), 85, 132.

4. Crossan, *God and Empire*, 28.

5. Ibid., 29.

6. Roger Haight, S.J., *Jesus Symbol of God* (Maryknoll, NY: Orbis Books, 1999), 338.

7. Barbara Fiand, *Awe-Filled Wonder: The Interface of Science and Spirituality* (Mahwah, NJ: Paulist Press, 2008), 68, 69.

8. Edward Schillebeeckx, *Christ: The Experience of Jesus as Lord*, trans. John Bowden (New York: Crossroad, 1981), 19, 20.

9. Fortunately the investigation was eventually and somewhat unexpectedly terminated. As is often the case, little is known of *precisely* why, in spite of what is being reported.

10. Dietrich Bonhoeffer, *Mystery of Holy Night,* ed. Manfred Weber; trans. Peter Heinegg (New York: Crossroad, 1996), 14.

11. Borg and Crossan, *The First Christmas,* 150.

12. Ibid., 144.

3. My Soul Rejoices

1. Nancy Schreck, OSF, and Maureen Leach, OSF, *Psalms Anew: In Inclusive Language* (Winona, MN: Saint Mary's Press, 1986), 16. Reprinted with permission.

2. Dietrich Bonhoeffer, *Mystery of Holy Night,* 6. The Magnificat is a singular attestation—mentioned only in Luke. Its significance, as I see it, is therefore primarily in what it tells us about how Luke saw Mary and, in the light of the Christmas parables discussed earlier, who the God of Jesus is for.

3. Richard P. McBrien, *Catholicism,* 2 vols. (Minneapolis, MN: Winston Press, 1980), 2:866–72.

4. See Joan Chittister, *Women, Ministry and the Church* (Ramsey, NJ: Paulist Press, 1983), 6, 7. This is an early, but still relevant, reflection of what continues to be a major ecclesial blind spot. Chrysostom's statement as cited by Chittister claims: "Among all savage beasts none is found so harmful as woman."

5. Barbara Fiand, *Wrestling with God: Religious Life in Search of Its Soul* (New York: Crossroad, 1996), 77–133. Also, Barbara Fiand, *Refocusing the Vision: Religious Life into the Future* (New York: Crossroad, 2002), 104–61.

6. For an extensive study of the history of dualism as it relates to our understanding of human sexuality and Christianity's rejection of women, see Uta Ranke Heinemann, *Eunuchs for the Kingdom of Heaven: Women, Sexuality, and the Catholic Church,* trans. Peter Heinegg (New York: Doubleday, 1990).

7. Only John mentions Mary's presence there. The Synoptic Gospels speak of women watching from a distance but do not mention Mary. Since the kind of proximity to someone crucified that is suggested by John very likely was not permitted, and since his is

the only attestation referring to the presence of the disciple John and Mary, this account is very likely parabolic rather than factual. In that sense it speaks with great compassion and deep symbolism about the kind of woman Mary was.

8. I borrowed the inscription for my homemade cards from Lucy's Cards, by Lucy Abrams, which I had first seen at the Los Angeles Education Conference Exhibition Center in Anaheim, California.

9. See Barbara Fiand, *Releasement: Spirituality for Ministry*; *Embraced by Compassion: On Human Longing and Divine Response*; and *On Becoming Who We Are: Passionate Musings in the Winter of Life*. All three books were published by the Crossroad Publishing Co. (New York), in 1987, 1993, and 2013 respectively.

10. Fiand, *Releasement*, 4–10.

11. Ibid., 6. It is clear that the symbology here belongs to the Middle Ages when a woman's part in procreation (the ovum was discovered in 1826) was not as yet realized and receptivity was seen as her only role.

12. Ibid.

13. Ibid.

14. Bonhoeffer, *Mystery of Holy Night*, 19.

15. Ibid., 18.

4. The Experience of Presence

1. Rainer Maria Rilke, "Wer seines Lebens viele Widersinne," *The Book of a Monastic Life*, taken from *Rilke's Book of Hours* (New York: Riverhead Books, 2005), 77 (my translation).

2. The above examples were taken from citations in Aniella Jaffé, *The Myth of Meaning: Jung and the Expansion of Consciousness* (New York: Penguin Books, 1975), 34–36.

3. This quote is found on the jacket of Bruce Lipton's book *Biology of Belief: Unleashing the Power of Consciousness, Matter & Miracles* (Santa Rosa, CA: Mountain of Love/Elite Books, 2005).

4. I make these observations not arbitrarily, because, of late, there seem to be other occasions that make one wonder about the apparently still prevalent disregard for women's intelligence. The case of the LCWR is just one example. The Sacred Congrega-

tion's order that there be episcopal supervision and ultimate permission as to what speakers are invited to LCWR events cannot be understood as anything other than demeaning. So also are the remarks reportedly made about this issue by Cardinal Müller: "we are not hostile to women and do not want to eat a woman every day! Without a doubt we have different understandings of religious life. We hope to help them rediscover their identity"(*L'Osservatore Romano*). Why is it in the first place that the cardinal thinks women religious in the United States have lost their identity and need the help of cardinals and bishops to rediscover it? On what evidence does he base this opinion? The high-level episcopal meetings in Rome to discuss "Women's Cultures: Equality and Difference" (February 4–7, 2015) attended only by bishops and cardinals in mostly closed door sessions but with some women advisors who had no vote is another recent example that gives one serious pause.

5. This should not be mistaken for a pantheistic view that *identifies* God with creation. It is rather a view that sees divine "energy" as suffusing creation, as holding it and empowering it to be. The world does not equal God. Rather God allows the world to be, sustains it and empowers it with God's presence (panentheism).

6. Pierre Teilhard de Chardin, *Pierre Teilhard de Chardin: Writings. Selected with an Introduction by Ursula King,* Modern Spiritual Masters Series (Maryknoll, NY: Orbis Books, 1999), 43.

7. Ibid., 42.

8. Barbara Fiand, *Embraced by Compassion: On Human Longing and Divine Response* (New York: Crossroad, 1993), 16.

9. Fritjof Capra, *The Tao of Physics* (New York: Bantam Books, 1977), xv.

10. Ken Wilber, *No Boundary: Eastern and Western Approaches to Personal Growth* (Boston: Shambala, 1979), 2.

11. Ibid., 3.

12. For an extensive discussion on this topic see ibid., chapter 2.

13. Francis Thompson (1859–1907), "The Hound of Heaven."

14. Fiand, *Embraced by Compassion,* 29.

15. Fiand, *Releasement: Spirituality for Ministry,* xi.

16. Karl Rahner, *A Rahner Reader,* ed. Gerald A. McCool (New York: Crossroad, 1984), 186, 187.

17. Fiand, *Embraced by Compassion,* 118.

18. Ibid.

19. Wilber, *No Boundary*, 5.

20. Willigis Jäger, *Mysticism for Modern Times: Conversations with Willigis Jäger*, ed. Christoph Quarch; trans. Paul Shepherd (Liguori, MO: Liguori/Triumph, 2006), xxii.

21. Ibid.

22. Ralph Harper, *On Presence: Variations and Reflections* (Philadelphia: Trinity Press International, 1991), 7.

23. Fiand, *Embraced by Compassion*, 112.

24. Wilber, *No Boundary*, 5.

25. Matthew Fox, ed., *Meditations with Meister Eckhart* (Santa Fe, NM: Bear & Company, 1982), 50.

26. Ibid.

27. Teilhard de Chardin,*Writings*, 23 (commentary by Ursula King).

28. Ibid.

29. Ibid., 49–51 (citation by Teilhard and concluding commentary by Ursula King).

30. Ibid., 52.

31. Willigis Jäger, *Search for the Meaning of Life: Essays and Reflections on the Mystical Experience* (Liguori, MO: Triumph Books, 1995), 235.

32. Wilber, *No Boundary*, 31 (my italics).

33. Ibid., 37.

34. Ibid., 38.

35. Ibid., 38–39.

36. Sir Arthur Eddington, in *Quantum Questions: Mystical Writings of the World's Great Physicists,* ed. Ken Wilber (Boston: Shambala Publications, 1985), citation on back cover.

37. Ken Wilber, ed., "Introduction: Of Shadows and Symbols," in *Quantum Questions: Mystical Writings of the World's Great Physicists* (Boston: Shambala Publications, 1985), 10, 11.

38. Barbara Fiand, *Awe-Filled Wonder: The Interface of Science and Spirituality* (Mahwah, NJ: Paulist Press, 2008), 33–34

39. Brian Swimme, *The Hidden Heart of the Cosmos: Humanity and the New Story* (Maryknoll, NY: Orbis Books, 1996), 100.

40. Ervin Laszlo, *Science and the Akashic Field: An Integral Theory of Everything* (Rochester, VT: Inner Traditions, 2004), 140.

41. Ervin Laszlo, *The Self-Actualizing Cosmos: The Akasha Revolution in Science and Human Consciousness* (Rochester, VT: Inner Traditions, 2014), 26.

42. Ibid., 90.

43. Ibid., 93.

44. My reflections were based largely on Bernard J. Boelen's work *Personal Maturity: The Existential Dimension* (New York: Seabury Press, 1978).

45. For a brief description of a number of ancient as well as contemporary theories, see Laszlo, *Science and the Akashic Field*, 151, 152

46. Ibid.

47. Ibid., 153.

48. Ibid.

49. Ibid.

50. Thich Nhat Hanh, *Living Buddha, Living Christ* (New York: Riverhead Books, 1995), 73.

5. Be What You See, Become What You Are

1. Oriah Mountain Dreamer, *The Invitation* (New York: HarperCollins Publishers, 1999), 12.

2. Robert Mickens, "Letter from Rome," *Commonweal Magazine,* February 18, 2015.

3. Bernard Cooke, *The Future of Eucharist: How a New Self-awareness among Catholics Is Changing the Way They Believe and Worship* (Mahwah, NJ: Paulist Press, 1997), 53.

4. John Dominic Crossan, *The Historical Jesus: The Life of a Mediterranean Jewish Peasant* (New York: HarperCollins Publishers, 1991), 262.

5. Ibid.

6. Ibid., 263.

7. McBrien, *Catholicism,* 2:588.

8. Crossan, *The Historical Jesus,* 399.

9. Ibid., 398.

10. Ibid.

11. Ibid., 399 (my italics).

12. Cooke, *Future of Eucharist,* 25.

13. Kenan B. Osborne, O.F.M., *Christian Sacraments in a Postmodern World: A Theology for the Third Millennium* (Mahwah, NJ: Paulist Press, 1999), 8.

14. Ibid., 8–9.

15. McBrien, *Catholicism*, 2:803.

16. Crossan, *The Historical Jesus*, 360–67.

17. Tad W. Guzie, S.J., *Jesus and the Eucharist* (New York: Paulist Press, 1974), 115.

18. Ibid.

19. Ibid.

20. Edward Schillebeeckx, *The Eucharist* (London: Sheed & Ward, 1968), 122–23.

21. Guzie, *Jesus and the Eucharist*, 78.

22. For one explanation see Herbert Haag, *Upstairs Downstairs: Did Jesus Want a Two-Class Church?* (New York: Crossroad, 1997), 81–98. For an abbreviated explanation, see Barbara Fiand, *On Becoming Who We Are: Passionate Musings in the Winter of Life* (New York: Crossroad, 2013), 107–9.

23. Robert J. Daly, S.J., "Sacrifice Unveiled or Sacrifice Revised: Trinitarian and Liturgical Perspectives," *Theological Studies* 64 (2003): 27.

24. I use the word "symbol" in the sense discussed in chapter 4. Symbols are not merely signs that "refer to" or "give instructions." Religious symbols are intended to help approximate the sacred for us in our present reality, to enable us to move into sacred space and, in that way, to open up a unitary experience that brings together the experiential/literal and the mystery that is beyond ordinary understanding. They are meant to make accessible what "in its own reality" defies expression.

25. The communion wafer is not helpful here. It not only distracts from the symbol of "bread broken," with the use of a different wafer for each recipient, but one is also hard pressed to recognize the "bread" with something that looks more like plastic.

26. See Augustine, Sermon 272: "and you must be the body of Christ to make that Amen take effect."

27. Daly, "Sacrifice Unveiled," 35.

28. Ibid., 36.

29. Ibid.

30. Ibid., 37 (my italics).

31. The latest data from the Pew Research Center shows that the share of all Catholics who say they attend Mass at least once a week has dropped from 47 percent in 1974 to 24 percent in 2012.

32. Edward Schillebeeckx, *The Eucharist,* 104.

33. Ibid., 121.

6. I Know That My Redeemer Lives

1. Nancy Heuck Johanson, *Light Showings: Moments in Divine Presence* (Bradenton, FL: BookLocker.com, 2013), 31–35. Nancy Johanson is a poet and a seer. The essays in this book speak of sacred moments in her life. Reprinted with permission.

2. John Dominic Crossan, *God and Empire: Jesus against Rome, Then and Now* (New York: HarperCollins, 2007), 95 (my italics).

3. McBrien, *Catholicism,* 2:412.

4. Roger Haight, S.J., *Spirituality Seeking Theology* (Maryknoll, NY: Orbis Books, 2014), 133 (my italics).

5. Marcus J. Borg, *Jesus: Uncovering the Life, Teachings, and Relevance of a Religious Revolutionary* (New York: HarperCollins, 2006), 43.

6. Haight, *Spirituality Seeking Theology,* 132 (my italics).

7. Ibid., 138.

8. Hans Küng, *Does God Exist? An Answer for Today* (New York: Vintage Books, 1981), 678.

9. Ibid., 678, 679.

10. McBrien, *Catholicism,* 2:405 (my italics).

11. Hans Küng, *On Being a Christian* (New York: Image Books, 1984), 382.

12. Herbert Haag, *Upstairs, Downstairs: Did Jesus Want a Two-Class Church?* (New York: Crossroad, 1998), 81, 82, 87–90.

13. According to scripture scholar Bart D. Ehrman, Paul already interpreted the crucifixion of Jesus as atonement for *our* sins (not yet original sin). He wanted to understand why Jesus, who was innocent, had been crucified. His explanation was that Jesus could not have been punished for his sins since his resurrection clearly showed that he was favored by God and would have been sinless.

Jesus must, therefore, have taken on our sins and atoned for them. See Bart D. Ehrman, *Peter, Paul, and Mary Magdalene: The Followers of Jesus in History and Legend* (New York: Oxford University Press, 2006), 113, 114.

14. Haight, *Spirituality Seeking Theology*, 137.

15. Ibid.

16. John Dominic Crossan, *Jesus: A Revolutionary Biography* (New York: HarperCollins, 1994), 181.

17. Ibid., 183 (my italics).

18. McBrien, *Catholicism*, 2:406–7.

19. Ibid.

20. Haight, *Spirituality Seeking Theology*, 134.

21. Borg, *Jesus*, 288.

22. Ibid., 286.

About the Author

Barbara Fiand is a Sister of Notre Dame de Namur. She is a retired professor of Spiritual and Philosophical Theology and has written nine previous books with The Crossroad Publishing Company. She gives retreats and workshops throughout the country and abroad on issues related to Holistic Spirituality, the Transformation of Consciousness, Human Maturation and the True Self, Prayer and the Quest for Healing, Spirituality and the New Science, as well as on the topics addressed in the present book. She lives in Cincinnati, Ohio.